HIGH NET WORTH INVESTING

HOW TO GROW YOUR WEALTH THROUGH PRACTICAL ASSET ALLOCATION

Sam Phoen

Marshall Cavendish
Business

© 2016 Sam Phoen and Marshall Cavendish International (Asia) Pte Ltd

Published in 2016 by Marshall Cavendish Business
An imprint of Marshall Cavendish International
1 New Industrial Road, Singapore 536196

Other Marshall Cavendish Offices:
Marshall Cavendish Corporation. 99 White Plains Road, Tarrytown NY 10591–9001, USA • Marshall Cavendish International (Thailand) Co Ltd. 253 Asoke, 12th Flr, Sukhumvit 21 Road, Klongtoey Nua, Wattana, Bangkok 10110, Thailand • Marshall Cavendish (Malaysia) Sdn Bhd, Times Subang, Lot 46, Subang Hi-Tech Industrial Park, Batu Tiga, 40000 Shah Alam, Selangor Darul Ehsan, Malaysia.

Marshall Cavendish is a trademark of Times Publishing Limited

National Library Board, Singapore Cataloguing-in-Publication Data:
Name(s): Phoen, Sam.
Title: High Net Worth Investing : How to grow your wealth through practical asset allocation / Sam Phoen.
Description: Singapore : Marshall Cavendish Business, 2016.
Identifier(s): OCN 950473893 | ISBN 978-981-47-7106-1 (paperback)
Subject(s): LCSH: Asset allocation. | Portfolio management. | Finance, Personal.
Classification: DDC 332.6–dc23

Cover design: Benson Tan
Cover image: AlexLMX/Shutterstock.com

Printed in Singapore by Markono Print Media Pte Ltd

CONTENTS

I. ASSET CLASSES

II. COMMON HIGH NET WORTH & RETAIL PRODUCTS

III. PUTTING IT ALL TOGETHER

Preface

I HAVE INVESTED for the firms I worked for and for myself all my life. I have made money, I have lost money. I gained a lot of knowledge and insights in the process – especially when I lost money. It hurts, but it made me learn. Some lessons can only be learnt when they hurt us, but there are also lessons which can be learnt without going through the hard way.

Fortunately for me, I have had more joy than pain over the years. From a personal investment perspective, I have invested in equities, bonds, cash products, real estate, foreign exchange, private equity and hedge funds. I have also dabbled in many kinds of structured products linked to these asset classes.

Thanks to these experiences, I have often been approached by friends and colleagues for investment advice. I totally enjoy sharing these experiences, as I find that my thoughts are a lot clearer when I have to articulate my suggestions or recommendations to them. The frequent sharing prompted me to share my experiences with more people, hence the book.

This book is like a compilation of my investment knowledge and experience over the years. Obviously I can't be an expert in each and every topic I write about. I would like to thank my long-time friend Kenneth Yeo for sharing his vast experience and expertise in Private Equity investments, my friendly insurance specialist Joey Seah for vetting the Insurance Summary Table, my nephew Siu Yen Lo for assisting me with other possible cover designs, and my ex-colleague and co-founder of Call Levels Daniel Chia for helping me with the price charts. Most of all, I am particularly grateful to my family, friends and colleagues who have supported me along the way, and gave me the motivation to write the book.

It's my hope that after reading this book, every High Net Worth and retail investor will be able to navigate safely through mistakes that are avoidable, ask the right questions, and approach any potential investments with a more complete perspective. A perspective that your investment adviser may not sufficiently cover, a perspective that most investors would not normally think of, and a perspective where you know for sure what you are buying.

Sam Phoen
June 2016

Introduction

FINANCIAL PRODUCTS ARE evolving constantly, just as regulations have been evolving to better protect consumers and investors. Post global financial crisis, the investment landscape has improved, and retail investors in particular are much better protected, with many safeguards to ensure they are well-informed and a financial product's risk profile is suitable for them.

However, this is only the bare minimum required to protect a retail investor. The usual principle of *caveat emptor*, Latin for "let the buyer beware", is still crucial in any financial transaction, because the seller tends to have more information than the typical buyer. This is understandable as retail buyers are typically not professionals in finance, and thus will only have limited technical knowledge with respect to financial products.

This book does not teach concepts of finance like those taught in Finance 101 in university. It does not cover complex mathematical formulas for calculating the fair value of financial products, as most of us would be lost halfway through. It also does not tell you what to buy or what not to buy.

This book attempts to help retail investors and high net worth individuals (HNWIs) understand in simple terms some of the common retail products available in the marketplace. It breaks down seemingly complex retail products into bite-size bits so investors can understand what they are buying. It helps investors think through whether what they are buying is indeed correctly expressing their own investment views. It also points out many less obvious pitfalls and considerations that are usually not highlighted by sellers of financial products.

Put another way, in the common analogy of teaching someone how to fish versus giving him a fish, this book certainly does not catch the fish for you. In all likelihood, you probably go fishing occasionally and know a little of how to fish already. This book identifies the rivers, lakes and oceans you could be fishing in and the kinds of fish available in each of them, helps you understand which of these fish may be suitable for you, and teaches you how to fish intelligently to achieve your target haulage.

Buying retail products should ideally not be a standalone or occasional decision. It should be deliberate and part of a well-thought-out investment plan. For example, what is the significance of a one-off 50% return on a $5,000 investment in a retail investment product when you have $500,000 that you leave in the current account uninvested? Would you achieve your bigger target with such ad hoc random return?

To formulate a proper investment plan that meets your investment needs, your entire investable assets should be considered in totality. A plan that matches your investment objectives and risk appetite should be drawn up such that a holistic approach to investment may be designed and implemented over time. This involves what financial planners traditionally call "asset allocation".

Asset allocation plans for retail investors and HNWIs are usually rather standardised in textbooks. Most financial literature has several cookie-cutter types of investment plans depending on one's age and income. The biggest drawback of these plans is that they usually only work if one has a few million dollars in the bank, but not when one only has a few hundred thousand, or less. These plans do not consider the practical difficulties when one is investing a much smaller capital amount. They also do not explain how two similar people with the same age and income may end up with very different investment strategies as each might have very different needs and risk appetites. This book hopes to demystify some of these big concepts and suggest a practical approach to individuals intending to achieve their dreams through appropriate planning and investing.

To help retail investors and HNWIs appreciate the different financial assets available in the market in simple terms, this book will start by describing in brief all the asset classes that are accessible by individuals currently. With some basic understanding of them, readers will be able to better appreciate the common retail products available in the market, and consider if and when the products could be used to their advantage. Finally I will put all these together and share how you can draw up a simple asset allocation plan to secure your financial future.

Part I

ASSET CLASSES

CHAPTER 1

Traditional
Asset Classes

THE THREE TRADITIONAL asset classes that most investors are familiar with are Equities (or stocks, as they are more
commonly called), Fixed Income (or bonds) and Cash/Cash
Equivalents (or money market instruments).

Equities probably need little introduction, as most
people would have bought or sold stocks before, or at least
hear a lot about it. Fixed Income or bonds are slightly less
popular compared to stocks, as these typically low-yielding
instruments are not "sexy" enough for high net worth investors to get excited about. There are thousands of books out
there dedicated to describing in great detail each of these two
asset classes. I will not attempt to duplicate their work here,
but will describe briefly what they are, in sufficient detail for
retail and high net worth investors to be able to appreciate
their key characteristics, so that they can better assess if these
assets should constitute part of their portfolio.

As for cash, most people may think they are just deposits in bank accounts. The truth is it could be a little more

sophisticated than that. I will also spend a little time to describe what one could do with their cash in hand.

EQUITIES

Equities, more commonly called stocks or shares, simply represent the share of ownership in listed companies. This ownership does not come with liabilities. Put another way, equity is the value of assets owned by the company after deducting the value of its liabilities.

An equity holder's claim on the company's assets ranks after creditors and bond holders. In other words, in the event of a company going bankrupt, its creditors and bond holders will get whatever money it has first, before its equity owners are paid. As such, equities are sometimes thought of as the riskiest of the three traditional asset classes. As risks and rewards are usually positively correlated, one would expect also to be rewarded well when the underlying company makes money. In fact, historically equities have tended to outperform both fixed income and cash or cash equivalents in the long run, hence their attraction for many investors.

By owning shares in a listed company, you are essentially a part owner of the business, have certain voting rights, and stand to gain when the company does well. Investors own shares of publicly listed companies for two main reasons: capital gain from the shares appreciating in value, and dividends. Over the long run, it has been shown that equities tend to do better than bonds and cash.

There are two types of stocks you could purchase from a stock exchange:

❖ Ordinary Shares – this is by far the most common form of shares we buy and sell on a stock exchange. It gives the owner some voting rights and a share of the profit after the company has met its other obligations. Profit is shared usually by dividends declared by the company.

❖ Preferential Shares – these shares do not carry any voting rights. The owner of these shares is preferred over the ordinary shares owners in the sense that the share of profit is distributed to them first, before the ordinary shareholders. Similarly, if a company goes bust, preferential shareholders will be paid before the ordinary shareholders. As such, they are slightly less risky than ordinary shares and sometimes get paid a slightly lower dividend rate.

Stocks are traded on Exchanges. There are many different exchanges in the world, the common ones being the New York Stock Exchange (NYSE), National Association of Securities Dealers Automated Quotations (NASDAQ), Tokyo Stock Exchange (TSE), London Stock Exchange (LSE), Shanghai Stock Exchange (SSE), Hong Kong Stock Exchange (HKEx), and many other country exchanges. They each have different listing rules, for example some admit only companies with good track records while others allow promising new firms to be listed.

Each of these exchanges usually has one or more indices created to track the collective performance of selected stocks listed on them. These indices are therefore useful for tracking a particular country or segment's stocks' performances and also serve as benchmarks for judging a fund manager's performance. Common indices include the S&P 500, which tracks 500 large stocks listed on the NYSE and NASDAQ; the Nikkei 225, tracking 225 top-rated Japanese companies listed on TSE; and the FTSE 100, tracking the largest 100 stocks listed in the UK.

Valuing Equities

Stock prices are affected by how a company is performing, and that predominantly means earnings and growth. To gauge a company's earnings trend and quality, as well as its growth potential, it is best to analyse the company's balance sheet, income statement and cash flow statement thoroughly. In general, an established company with a long-term track record would be looked favourably upon if it could show stable earnings growth, even if growth is small. For a relatively new company, the growth of sales and revenue would be much higher, even if net earnings may not be positive. The speed at which it is adding customers would also be heavily scrutinised to determine its future growth potential, especially for IT-related companies.

A popular valuation tool for equities is the Discounted Cash Flow (DCF) valuation. It attempts to value a company based on a projection of the company's future cash flows/ earnings/dividends, discounted by the time value of money, using typically the company's weighted average cost of capital. Essentially, it is the sum of all future cash flows represented in present value. Sounds simple, but it isn't, because there are a lot of assumptions to be made to make this valuation method meaningful. As such, it tends to be used only by the professionals and seldom used by retail investors.

For retail investors who find DCF valuation a tad too difficult, there are slightly easier comparative valuation tools to use. Some of the more common valuation ratios are:

◆ Price to Earnings (P/E)

◆ Price to Book Value (P/B)

◆ Price to Free Cash Flow (P/FCF)

One should compare not just the absolute value of the ratio, but also relative to its own past, relative to its industry peers, as well as relative to the broader market to have a more objective assessment of the cheapness or expensiveness of the stock. Even then, remember that the ratios are only a snapshot of what the stock price is relative to some accounting numbers. There are many things that go into these accounting numbers, but a lot more information is also not reflected in these numbers. Qualitative assessment of the company, like its strategy and target markets and customers, is just as important for getting a more complete valuation and assessment of the stock.

Besides the above quantitative and qualitative assessments of a company, collectively known as Fundamental Analysis normally, one could also look at it from a technical perspective, that is, by charts. Technical Analysis is based on looking at movements of the price and volume of the underlying stock. Traders who are predominantly trend-lovers would trade with the momentum, while mean-reversion believers would trade against the momentum.

My preferred way of valuing a stock is a combination of both Fundamental and Technical Analysis. I tend to use fundamental analysis to sieve out the undervalued stocks, then use technical analysis to time my buying of the stock. Similarly, when the stock becomes overvalued over time based on my fundamental valuation, I would use the charts to decide when to sell to maximise my profit.

Investing in Equities

Buying a company's stock that is listed on a stock exchange is probably the simplest way to express a view on the company. Exchanges have different rules like lot size, trading hours, settlement cycle, tax, etc. Some exchanges like the US exchanges allow short selling, while other emerging market exchanges would have restrictions around short selling.

If researching and buying single stocks is not your cup of tea, or it is simply too tedious for your liking, or you are just happy to have exposure to a particular sector or market, you could consider buying into Exchange-Traded Funds or ETFs. ETFs are investment funds that are traded on the stock exchange. Stock ETFs track an index, like the S&P500 or a particular sector like pharmaceuticals. ETFs are popular because they are easily accessible, have good liquidity, charge low fees, and trade just like individual stocks, which most investors are familiar with.

The difficulty in equities investing is not just in choosing which stocks to buy. Deciding when to sell is sometimes even more challenging! For an investor driven by fundamental investing, the best time to sell is when the price of the stock exceeds the fair valuation of the stock by a reasonably large margin. What exactly is a "large" margin is sometimes best determined by one's risk appetite or by reference to the stock's historical valuation. For technical investors, on the other hand, whose actions are driven by chart patterns, deciding when to sell is easier. The most common mistake I see retail investors make is what legendary investor Peter Lynch described as "cutting the flowers and keeping the weeds", i.e. taking profit on stocks which had gone up in value, while holding on to stocks which are underwater. Over the long run, an investor in this mode will end up with only "weeds" or under-performing stocks – which is not the best investment outcome for the long run.

More sophisticated investors could also consider stock index futures or stock options. Both of these instruments allow you to bet on the underlying stock going up or down. However, as they are leverage products, use them with care as you could lose more than your principal if you are not careful with your money management.

FIXED INCOME

Fixed Income, more commonly known as bonds to the lay-person, are instruments that pay a fixed amount at a fixed schedule. The bonds represent debt for the company, and the yield is how much the company is paying the buyer of the bond (i.e. the lender) to lend the money to the company.

Typically, fixed interests or coupons are paid half-annu-ally, and the maturity or principal amount will be paid at the maturity date together with the final coupon payment. When a company issues a bond, it creates an obligation for it to pay the coupons and return the principal at maturity. If it misses a coupon payment, it would be said to be in default, and could potentially be forced into bankruptcy if it does not have sufficient cash flows to repay outstanding debts.

Bonds pay coupons in different ways, among which are these few key types:

- ◆ Fixed Coupon Bonds – By far the most common type, these pay a fixed percentage coupon through maturity.

- ◆ Variable Coupon Bonds – Coupons for these bonds are tied to a particular benchmark rate, like LIBOR, plus a spread.

- ◆ Inflation-Indexed Bonds – These bonds pay a "real rate" of interest that varies with the Consumer Price Index of a particular country.

- ◆ Zero-Coupon Bonds – These are bonds sold at a deep discount to the notional value and redeemed at full face value at maturity, which could be anything from six months to 30 years. Holders of these bonds do not receive any interest.

Most bonds are traded over-the-counter, and not listed on exchanges. There are exceptions though, like in China, where a small number of bonds are traded on the China stock exchange, while Retail Bonds are listed on the Singapore Exchange too. Here are the different issuers in the market, and what their bonds are called:

- ◈ Government – Government bonds (in own currency); Sovereign bonds (in foreign currencies); Treasury bonds (US government bonds)

- ◈ Province/state/municipality – Municipal bonds

- ◈ Government-backed agencies – Agency bonds

- ◈ Corporate – Corporate bonds

- ◈ Financial institutions – Financial bonds, or sometimes also generically called Corporate bonds

Besides the above, there are some other names used to denote bonds of different characteristics. The common ones include:

- ◈ Convertible Bonds – These bonds may be converted into the company's equity at or from a pre-determined time in the future, usually at the bond holder's discretion. Essentially, it is a corporate bond plus a stock option. Due to the ability to participate in the stock's appreciation, convertible bonds tend to pay a lower coupon.

- ◈ Asset-Backed Bonds – Bonds that are backed with assets are generically called asset-backed bonds. Mortgage-backed bonds are one sub-type, being backed by mortgage loans.

- ◈ Callable Bonds – Bonds that can be "called back" by the issuer at or after a certain pre-determined date. Companies tend to call back bonds when interest rates have fallen, as they could then refinance their debt at a lower interest rate.

⬥ Junk Bonds – These are bonds that are rated below "investment grade", which means their ratings are rated "BB" or lower by major rating agencies like S&P (Standard & Poor's). They are sometimes also referred to as "high yield" bonds as the issuer has to pay higher interest to compensate investors for the higher default risks.

Valuing Fixed Income

When a bond is first issued, it is usually at "par", which normally is $100 per unit. The price of a bond moves inversely with the interest rate, meaning if the price goes up, the yield falls and vice versa. The price of a bond is simply the value of future cash flows discounted back to today. Therefore if the interest rate goes up, discounting future cash flows with a higher rate would result in a lower price for the bond.

Very broadly, two factors impact the price of a bond:

⬥ Risk-free interest rate

⬥ Credit spread unique to the issuer

The risk-free interest rate typically refers to the equivalent-tenure government yield, and that varies with the broader state of the country's economy. When a country is doing well or inflation is running high, the risk-free rate tends to rise.

The credit spread that is unique to the issuer depends on how the issuer is faring. If a company is doing well, the credit spread tends to narrow, because the risk in owning the bond is lower. Conversely, if a company is hit by losses or bad press, the credit spread will widen because the market will expect to be compensated with a higher yield to hold on to the bond.

To figure out what a bond is yielding at a particular price, the most common measure is the yield-to-maturity (YTM). That is the effective annualised rate one should expect to receive until maturity for owning the bond. Most bonds by the same or different issuers have different maturities and coupons, making comparison difficult. YTM is thus a good way to compare these bonds.

A slight variation of the YTM is a Yield-to-Call (YTC), which applies to Callable Bonds. In this case, which typically happens when interest rates have fallen, the issuer may try to call back the bond (typically at par) as they could refinance or issue another new bond at lower yield, thus saving them some money. A Yield-to-Put (YTP) is yet another yield measure similar to the YTC, except that this time the holder of the bond has the right to "put back" the bond to the issuer on or after a certain date before the maturity date. In both the YTC and YTP cases, as there is a possibility and flexibility that the bond may not be held to maturity, investors must make an assessment of the likelihood of a call or put when deciding whether to buy the bond.

Another important concept in valuing bonds is the bond's duration. The most commonly used measures are Macaulay Duration and Modified Duration. They are, respectively, a measure of the weighted average time until all cash flows are received, and a measure of price sensitivity to yield changes. Macaulay Duration is measured in years, and a bond's duration would vary between 0 and the maturity date. A zero-coupon bond would have a Macaulay Duration equal to the maturity. Modified Duration measures the percentage change in price per unit of yield change.

The two duration measures are quite similar numerically. For example, a two-year bond trading at par may have a Macaulay Duration a little under two years, and a Modified Duration of just under 2%. What this means is that the longer the duration, the more sensitive it would be to changes in yield. In a rising interest rate environment, one would be better off in shorter-duration bonds as a rise in yield would hurt the bond price less. In a falling interest rate environment, having long-duration bonds would help one to make more from potential price gains. Intuitively, when rates are rising, your bond price will fall, and a bond with shorter duration would suffer less as it is nearer maturity than another bond with say 10 years more to maturity. As such, during periods of rising rates, investors tend to prefer "short duration", while periods of falling rates would see investors go "long duration".

Investing in Fixed Income

Unlike equities, it is not as easy to buy a bond, as the minimum nominal size is usually quite large, typically at $200,000. This puts it out of reach for most retail investors other than High Net Worth Individuals. Even if one has $400,000 to invest in bonds, one may not want to buy just two bonds as that means one is highly exposed to these two bonds and not well diversified. For this reason, unless one is happy with the lack of diversification or has a lot more investable cash, one would not be buying a bond directly. As bonds are traded OTC mostly, their prices are not as transparent. Banks and brokers may also charge a bigger bid-ask spread due to the illiquidity, especially with Corporate Bonds. Thus bonds are not meant to be traded regularly in and out for retail investors.

Buy-and-hold is a common strategy for retail investors when they come to investing in Fixed Income. However, there are occasions when one should consider selling one's bond holding too:

- ◆ Take profit – Typically when interest rates have fallen a lot, or in the case of a Convertible Bond, when the underlying stock has risen by a lot.

- ◆ Need principal for other needs – These may not be driven by economic considerations, for example when one needs cash for an emergency. But sometimes one may sell one's bond holding when the returns in other assets are far more compelling than holding on to a low-yield bond to maturity.

- ◆ Get out before it's too late – When you expect the price to fall more because there are a lot more interest rate hikes in the pipeline than the market has priced in; or when you think the credit-worthiness of the issuer is likely to deteriorate going forward.

There are other instruments that are more transparent and accessible to retail investors, like Retail Bonds, which trade at much smaller denominations, typically from $1,000, and also bond ETFs. Both are traded on stock exchanges, though they may not be available to all stock exchanges, only the more developed ones. Buying into bond funds or bond unit trusts is also popular among retail investors. Again, just like with equities, more sophisticated individuals could also consider bond index futures or options. Even though they are less volatile compared to equities, do use these leverage products with care as you could lose more than your principal.

CASH & CASH EQUIVALENTS

Besides the cash one has in the bank, what typically constitutes cash or cash equivalents from a retail investor's perspective includes Money Market Funds, Treasury Bills (T-bills), short-term Corporate Commercial Papers (CPs) and Certificates of Deposit (CDs). Essentially, anything that is liquid and can be easily converted into cash in a very short time could be considered in this category. From a business's balance sheet perspective, any high credit quality and highly liquid instrument that can be sold with little to no loss in value with maturities less than three months can be defined as a cash equivalent.

Here are the brief descriptions of some of the more common Cash Equivalents available to retail investors:

- Money Market Funds – funds that invest in short-term debt securities.

- Treasury Bills (T-bills) – short-term government securities, of maturity typically one year or less.

◆ Corporate Commercial Papers (CPs) – short-term securities issued by a corporation, typically of maturity no more than 270 days.

◆ Certificates of Deposit (CDs) – notes issued by a bank, of maturity one month to one year typically.

These short-term securities are actively traded in the Money Market, which is an inter-bank market where financial institutions borrow or lend to each other for a short period, usually less than 13 months. They are very liquid, and tend to come with much narrower bid-ask spread. As they are generally issued by the government or banks or corporations of good credit standing, their yields are generally very low too, especially when compared to stocks. However, they usually pay a little more than bank interest from a retail perspective, and are hence worth learning more about.

In addition to the above more sophisticated instruments, there are also short-dated time deposits (TD) which retail investors could use to improve their yield. While time deposits are not flexible in terms of instant access to liquidity, one could always break up one's deposit amounts into different maturing tenures, so as to ensure that one always has some cash coming due every month for use. For example, if one has $180,000 to place in time deposit, one could consider breaking this up into 12 × $15,000 and placing each chunk in a different TD, with one maturing every month. The worst case for TD is forgoing the interest that one would earn if one needs to withdraw before maturity, but if it is infrequent, then time deposits are still a worthwhile consideration as the principal is protected even in an early withdrawal.

Besides time deposits, banks sometimes do offer principal-protected structured deposits (SDs) too. An SD is really a deposit plus an option. As most SDs have a fixed maturity date, the short-dated ones can also be considered as cash equivalents. They function like time deposits, except that they come with a small amount of risk in that the investor may earn a higher interest if certain conditions come true and earn no interest if otherwise. SDs are covered in more detail in Chapter 7.

Valuing Cash / Cash Equivalents

Most of the short-dated Cash Equivalents mentioned have a maturity of up to a year. They are usually issued at a discount to par value, which means the investor buys it below $100, for example, and receives $100 at maturity. Due to the short tenure, it makes valuing them rather straightforward. So unlike valuing bonds, which have a series of cash flows, these short-term debt instruments have just one cash flow at maturity, making complex valuation formulas unnecessary.

The easiest way is simply to compare the annualised yields offered by the different instruments, paying attention in particular to the issuer and unique features of each. One of the most important differentiations of yield is the credit-worthiness of the issuers. Consider if the additional yield pick-up offered for corporate issues over Treasuries is worth the additional risk you take on, no matter how small it is. Differing features can also result in different yields, like a call feature on a CD, for example.

In normal times, the yield curve is positively sloping, meaning the longer the tenure, the higher the interest rate.

That happens because one sacrifices liquidity, and so one is compensated for it. Therefore, one would normally expect to be paid a few basis points higher for slightly longer tenure.

Investing in Cash / Cash Equivalents

Keeping cash in a bank account is clearly the most liquid form of all cash assets. However, that comes with some opportunity cost, as interest rates in a current or savings account are really low. If one only needs say $10,000 at short notice most times, but has a total of $50,000 in the bank account, one should consider deploying the other $40,000 to better use in some cash equivalents.

Many cash equivalents, like T-bills, are not easily accessible to retail investors, as they usually have fairly large minimum dealing sizes. As such, the easiest way is to entrust your "excess" cash that you don't need that frequently to a Money Market Fund. There are many such funds in the market, and most allow access to your cash in a day or two. The funds will in turn invest in short-term debt instruments on your behalf, while charging you a small management fee and some performance fee. For more information on choosing money market funds, please read Chapter 8 on Unit Trusts.

As mentioned earlier, breaking up excess cash into different chunks and placing them in time deposits or structured deposits of varying tenures is another way to maximise your returns. This is less flexible as compared to a money market fund, but certainly yields more than current or savings accounts. So time deposits could form part of your allocation within your cash / cash equivalents portion.

Conclusion

Stocks, bonds and cash are the three most common asset classes in any investment literature. As most people are somewhat familiar with them, this chapter has only attempted to cover the most basic concepts of each. Armed with this knowledge, one should be able to comprehend the advantages and disadvantages of investing in each of them.

Going beyond these three traditional asset classes, there are other asset classes which are increasingly popular as the investing public gets more sophisticated and demands more alternatives, especially the higher-yielding variety. Some of these alternatives include Real Estate, Foreign Exchange, Commodities, Hedge Funds and Private Equity. These will be discussed in the coming chapters.

CHAPTER 2

Real Estate

As investors look for alternative asset classes to diversify into, Real Estate is increasingly gaining in popularity, especially in Asia. Investors like it as it is tangible, seen as a good inflation hedge, has reasonable yield when rented out, and most importantly, has good potential for capital appreciation. The main downside to Real Estate is its illiquidity and the need for large capital outlay. As such, one needs to have a long-term perspective when investing in real estate, and by long-term I mean several years at the minimum.

As I will cover real estate from the retail perspective, the focus will largely be on residential properties. Other types of real estate that may be interesting to more wealthy individuals include commercial and industrial properties. The basic analysis for all property types is rather similar, so one can use what we will discuss here for residential properties and apply it to commercial and industrial properties. However, as commercial and industrial properties tend to involve more sophisticated players like private and public companies, one should be aware that the resources and information an individual has compared to these companies may not be equal.

As such, a retail investor dabbling in these properties should exercise even more care and do more due diligence in order not to be run over by these more informed investors.

This chapter covers real estate from the perspective of buying for investment purposes, which would typically involve renting it out for income. Buying a property to live in entails slightly different considerations from buying for investment. For example, rental yield would appear to be irrelevant if one buys to live in and has no intention of ever renting the property out. However, it is still worth bearing in mind as one may eventually want to move to another place and need to sell or rent out the old home. The next buyer could be buying to live in or for investment, and you can be sure that he will scrutinise your home and probably apply the evaluation criteria that I will outline in this chapter to your home. Thus, whether you are buying to live in or for investment, you might want to apply the same evaluation criteria that I will outline here for investment properties.

Factors Affecting Real Estate Prices

"Location, location, location" is often quoted to be the three most important factors for real estate. While location is clearly extremely important, that alone is not sufficient to help one make a wise investment decision. There are many other factors we need to consider alongside location too. Here are some factors which I think are important:

- ◆ Location
- ◆ Physical attributes
- ◆ Tenure

- Price
- Interest rate
- Yield
- Affordability
- Redevelopment potential
- Market trend
- Other factors

Let's discuss each of them in a little more detail here.

(a) Location

One usually thinks that this is so obvious that it is a no-brainer. When one thinks that, one is usually thinking of say the distance to the nearest underground/metro station, being situated in a safe neighbourhood, near the central business district or the main shopping belt, etc. These are important considerations and should be considered, but people who only consider these factors would be missing the big picture.

One should remember that real estate is a long-term investment, not necessarily for one's own staying in, and that means it need not be restricted to one's city or even country of domicile. From a top-down perspective, one should first decide on which country, then city, then district, then the street and finally the unit itself.

Country or sovereign risk is probably the single biggest risk in any property investment. Think about it: what is the point of getting the best property in the best location in a country that is headed downhill? From an investment perspective, there is nothing worse than buying a property in a country sinking both economically and politically. History has shown that property prices there tend not to appreciate, not to mention the likely sliding value of the country's currency.

If one is positive about a country, then go for the capital city, if possible, unless one is very familiar with the lesser-known fringe cities. Very often, the capital city is way pricier in comparison, but there is good reason for that, because that's where the bulk of the economic activities are carried out, and so it tends to attract the best talents from the rest of the country and even overseas. With that, the demand for property there is naturally higher than in other cities, which may conversely see the hollowing out of talents and in the long run an underperforming real estate market.

The district to pick depends on what one prefers. For the most "rentability", one should usually be near the central business district or the touristy areas. Alternatives might be areas with good amenities or good schools. At this juncture, one should consider the usual "micro" factors of location, e.g. accessibility, distance to public transport, safety of the surrounding neighbourhood, future development plans, the list goes on. Many of these are really common sense, but do remember this: consider what others might need, not just what you like, and you should be fine. You are not buying to live in the property yourself, so what others may need is way more important than your individual tastes.

(b) Physical Attributes

The physical appearance of a property is very important. For a flat or apartment in a condominium or a gated development, the facilities available and the upkeep of the common facilities go a long way in influencing one's first impression, as one would see the common areas before seeing the individual unit. For a house, the equivalent would be the upkeep of the external facade, the car porch and its surrounding garden and/or pool, etc.

The interior matters a lot too. The important attributes to consider are size, layout, number of bedrooms and bathrooms, heating/air-conditioning, etc. Some attributes can be changed, while others can't. For a flat, the layout is usually fixed and similar across different floors for units of the same "stack" in a building. While the interior could be changed somewhat to suit one's tastes, there are pros and cons to doing so. For example, if you like big bedrooms and merge two bedrooms into one, bear in mind that it might reduce the rent in some cities as many developed cities place more importance on number of bedrooms instead of size. For some cities in cold climates, having central heating or floor heating may be absolutely essential. In tropical climates air-conditioning is crucial. Of course one could install these things after buying the flat/house, but that may cost a fortune depending on the extent of work to run the pipes, so one needs to factor that into consideration.

Some other points to note include the direction that the main door, living room and bedrooms are facing, and also flat/house number. Depending on whom you think you want to appeal to for rental, you need to have different considerations. For example, Westerners don't mind the afternoon sun shining into the living room as much as people from the East. People from China tend to prefer a North-South orientation for their home. There are some cultures who absolutely hate selected numbers. For example, Chinese from Southern China tend to avoid the number 4, because it sounds similar to "death" in the Chinese language. Westerners dislike the number 13 for they consider it unlucky. If it can be avoided, try not to buy a flat or house having an "inauspicious" number.

Finally, when it comes to internal renovation of the flat or house, be mindful again of whom you want to rent it out to. It usually does not pay to be too elaborate, as everyone has different tastes, not to mention that it will cost you more to renovate it with fancy fittings. Neutral palettes and moveable furniture instead of built-in will give you more flexibility to change to fit tenants' preferences.

(c) Tenure

The tenure of the property you buy determines how long you can own the property. This varies from country to country, and also within a country. For example, typical residential properties in China come with 70-year leases. In the UK and Singapore, it could vary from a starting tenure of 99 years to 999 years to forever (known as Freehold or Estate in Fee Simple).

All things being equal, the longer the tenure, the pricier it tends to get. To some people, even a remaining tenure of say 50 years may be sufficient as they do not anticipate living past the expiry of the tenure. For others, it may be important to have a long tenure so that they can pass the property on to their dependants.

Which tenure should you buy? There is no simple answer there, as the answer depends on many factors like your preference, your budget, your usage plan, your desired yield, etc. Suffice it to say that if two properties are identical in every way except the tenure, and they command the same price, go for the property with the longer tenure, as you will get more cash flow from the longer tenure.

Besides affecting the value, the tenure of a property may also impact the willingness of a financial institution to finance it. If a property has a remaining tenure of 30 years, it may be hard to find banks willing to extend a mortgage as they may view the short-tenure property as a depreciating asset!

(d) Price

The price of the property wasn't the first thing I described as the most important factor in your decision. There is a price for everything, and until you know what you want or need, the price should be secondary to it. Imagine making a decision based first on price – i.e. looking for a property within your price budget or a supposed "under-priced" flat in the market – you might end up with a property that does not satisfy your needs.

The right approach is to first satisfy yourself based on the location, physical attributes and tenure minimally, then find a property within your desired price range that meets all or most of the factors you consider important. In that way, you are less likely to end up buying a property just because it is "cheap", but which is in a less ideal locale, or does not meet your other important considerations.

What then is the "right" price to pay for a property? In this digital age, many things are transparent and can be found on the internet if one tries hard enough. The general price level in a particular precinct should be available in most developed economies. One should use that as the basis for assessing whether the property one is looking at is expensive or cheap.

To compare across different developments, look at the price per square foot (psf) or per square metre (psm). This unit price can be used for comparison if the properties being compared are rather similar in nature or layout. If they are not, one should also adjust for the difference. For example, a penthouse unit of 150sqm comprising 100sqm of built-in area and another 50sqm of roof terrace would normally have a much lower psm price as compared to a fully built-in 150sqm flat in the same area.

If the property market is rising, the asking price of a property is usually higher than the last done price in that pre-cinct. The opposite may not be true for a falling market, so it is up to you to knock the price down if the trend is clearly down.

Before you buy, it is important to check with one or more banks the valuation of the property you intend to buy (to ensure you are not over-paying) and the amount you can borrow. Make sure you have the cash to pay for the first 20–30% of the property as banks' typical loan-to-value is about 70–80%, and even lower sometimes for investment properties.

The purchase of a property may be the single largest financial commitment that one makes, so it is crucial that you are 100% sure and comfortable that your offered purchase price is something you have researched and are confident is the right price. Until you are absolutely certain, do not make the purchase. If you have done sufficient research, you would generally feel happy when your offered price is accepted by the seller, instead of feeling jittery.

(e) Interest Rate

Almost everyone takes a mortgage loan from a bank when buying a property. Even if you have the entire purchase price in cash, it still usually doesn't make a lot of sense to buy a property entirely with cash. The reason is that liquidity in hand is really priceless, and one should try as much as possible to stay liquid, assuming the cost to do so is reasonable.

As such, the interest rate charged by the bank is very important, as it is something you have to live with for the entire period of your mortgage, which is usually 15 years or more. In a low interest rate environment, which we have been used to, it is easy to be lulled into complacency to think that the interest rate will never rise. As it rises, which it inevitably will during the life of your mortgage, you will find that the monthly repayment amount could rise very quickly too. To ensure that you can continue to afford the monthly mortgage repayment, you would do well not to over-extend yourself in buying that dream property.

There are many variations in banks' mortgages. The least you should do is to compare the rates and the features offered. Pick one that best matches your needs and views. For example, if you think that you could be selling your investment property within the next three years, do not pick a mortgage with a three-year "lock-in" period where you would be penalised if you redeem the mortgage when selling the property. Many mortgages are also pegged or linked to a "benchmark" rate, like the LIBOR or Time Deposit rate. If you are no expert in the interest rate market, the least you should ask is the history of the benchmark rate, and also the transparency of the rate. The more transparent the rate, the less likely it is for the bank to be able to change it at its whim and fancy.

(f) Yield

The yield of an investment property is defined as the annual rental income divided by the property price. The net yield is defined as the net rental income, after deducting all maintenance, tax and other charges related to the property, divided by the property price. The net yield can be directly compared with the interest rate you are paying to service your mortgage.

The least you should aim to achieve is for your net rental income to cover the interest repayment of your mortgage. Your monthly mortgage repayment would usually include repaying a part of your principal besides the interest charged, unless it is an interest-only mortgage available in some countries. Generally it is a tall order to expect the net rental income to fully cover the total principal plus interest repayment of your mortgage. If it does, and if the general property price trend is flat or higher, it is almost a no-brainer to be invested in property. Conversely, if the net rental doesn't even cover the interest payments, then the general property trend had better be up for it to make sense, otherwise you will suffer negative "carry" and subsidise your tenant with no apparent upside or reason!

So where do you find higher-yielding properties? Newer properties tend to command higher rental, but they also tend to cost more, so the net effect on yield varies, though in general the newer it is, the higher the yield. Longer-tenure properties are generally pricier than similar shorter-tenure properties, so yield tends to be poorer because tenants are not going to be paying more for your property which has 999 years remaining compared to one with 99 years remaining – it simply doesn't matter to them.

(g) Affordability

Affordability of property by the general population ultimately determines how high prices can go. If properties end up costing so much that only rich foreigners can afford to buy, it would certainly be a political hot potato and unsustainable for the long term. Due to the low interest rate environment globally in recent years, property prices have gone up in many major cities in the world.

While one could compare general price levels across different countries, that may not be the best indicator as the countries' varying stages of development and income levels render direct comparison rather arbitrary. As such, there are several ratios which we use to better compare affordability, including:

- ❖ Price-to-Income Ratio – the higher the ratio, the less affordable.

- ❖ Price-to-Rent Ratio – the higher the ratio, the higher the price and/or the lower the rent.

- ❖ Mortgage-to-Income Ratio – the higher the ratio, the less affordable.

By tracking these ratios, one can more objectively determine whether general price levels are too high compared to the past as well as across different countries, and whether current price levels are sustainable. Of course, the general affordability index is just a number to track whether prices are likely to rise further. It is not helpful if you can't afford a property you like irrespective of how low the affordability index is.

What is crucial in every individual's case is the ability to service the mortgage based on one's income and/or the potential rental income. For an investment property, it is important to ensure that the rent from the property covers minimally the mortgage interests. The rest of the monthly mortgage payment is ideally fully covered either by a small part of the investor's salary or from the rental income. To be safe, one should have enough reserves such that the monthly mortgage repayments could still be easily serviced should the property be vacant for several months.

(h) Redevelopment Potential

In general, it is much easier renting out a new property, even though the asking rental tends to be higher. Conversely, renting out an old property usually means lower rental as potential tenants tend to go for flashy new flats. As such, older properties tend to appeal to price-conscious people who may not need the modern facilities as much.

With the lower rent and yield, what then is the attraction from an investment perspective of an old property? Besides a lower purchase price than comparable new properties in the vicinity, some old properties also come with the potential of redevelopment. Redevelopment involves the tearing down of the existing old property and building a new one, usually at a much higher density. This is made possible typically when an area is zoned or earmarked for "regeneration" or rejuvenation for specific reasons. When this happens, the plot of land that the old property sits on tends to have its plot ratio increased. The plot ratio defines how densely the plot of land may be built up to. When it is increased, the total built-up area allowed by the zoning authorities is raised, and more units can thus be built – and sold – on the same plot of land.

When there is redevelopment potential, the value of the old property on that plot would naturally be worth more, provided of course it can be torn down and rebuilt. This would be a good time to monetise one's investment either by selling the property at a higher price, or selling collectively with the rest of the owners in the same plot of land to a developer. If and when this happens, the higher selling price should more than offset the low yield one suffers in all the years renting out at low value.

However, a word of caution is that just because a property is old does not mean that there is upside in price from redevelopment. The key is in the government's decision to upgrade a specific area and the corresponding increase in the plot ratio that usually accompanies it.

(i) Market Trend

Unless one is always on the pulse of the property market, it is sometimes difficult to know if the market is going up or down until it is widely reported in the news. When it is widely known, then most people would have one of these two attitudes:

◈ When the property market is trending down, everyone thinks that it will go lower, and so they tend to sit and wait.

◈ When prices are trending up, everyone hopes to buy it at the same price as last transacted or even lower, which almost never happens.

So when is the best time to buy? Just like stocks and other investment products, it is best to buy just before prices move up obviously, but most of us are not so sharp and quick to be able to spot it and buy before price rallies. Properties are illiquid, and every unit is different, so it is not easy to pull the trigger quickly when the time comes. What is important is thus to be engaged with the market, feel the sentiment on the ground, identify the areas you are interested in, and track transacted prices there and nearby.

Property investment is a huge investment, and you are only going to buy one after a long due diligence process, so don't rush! Only when you have seen enough properties would you be able to know exactly what you like or dislike, and only then would you recognise the right one when it comes along.

Why is market trend important? Besides the obvious of buying low and selling high, it matters hugely if you have a property to sell too. In a down trend, you might want to consider selling your property first before buying. In an up trend, you should consider buying first before selling your property, provided of course you have the funds to finance your purchase before selling. If you don't have a property to sell before buying, knowing the trend is also very relevant in helping you decide on the purchase price. So in general there are three scenarios to consider, and here are the recommended strategies in each of them.

When the market is trending down: Stay engaged with the market, and watch the transacted prices closely. The first sign of bottoming out is when there is an increase in transaction volume, and prices transacted are no longer much lower than the previous transaction. If you find the right property now, you could try to bid at a price lower than the last done price. This would provide some room to cushion against possible future price falls. If you are right that the market is at or near bottoming out, then you would have bagged yourself a bargain which you normally would not get when the market is trending up.

When the market is trending sideways, or directionless: This usually happens at turning points, but this could be a long dragged out affair that lasts for years too. If it is sideways after a big price rally, then one should be very careful, because the next trend might well be down, though it could also be consolidating for the next leg up. If it is sideways after an extended period of price falls, it may be time to assess whether the next trend might be back up or further down. If your assessment is that it is most likely to be up next, it would be a good time to actively look for your dream property now. A sideways market allows you to buy at stable prices, which is impossible in an upward trending market.

When the market is trending up: If you think it is the start of a big up trend, then it may be worthwhile buying your property now. However, you can be sure that you won't be the only one having that view when the trend is clear. So you would almost always have to pay more than the previous buyer, and that is not an easy trigger to pull because most of us do not like to buy "highs". If you have done your due diligence, and your dream property is available, you should have the confidence to pay slightly higher to buy it. I know it is extremely difficult, but if you are confident of your research and engagement in the past months or years, then have faith and stick to what you believe. This is why you have been engaged with the market all this while! It doesn't feel good to pay more than others, but it feels worse if you are proven right subsequently but you didn't buy!

With property transaction information and related research more readily available nowadays, identifying a trend early is not as difficult as in the past. While it may not be easy to be ahead of a trend turning, it is not as difficult to identify an up move once it appears to have started. Knowing the trend, or more importantly having a view of the trend going forward, would enable you to pull the trigger with much more confidence.

(j) Other Factors

There are other factors that may not be avoidable or not applicable to everyone but apply specifically to individual circumstances. Some of these factors include:

- ◈ Tax: The tax regime varies from country to country. Rental income is taxable in most countries. Stamp duty is also a fixture everywhere, with some countries taxing non-residents more to clamp down on foreigners over-speculating in domestic real estate. Some countries also impose

tax on capital gains, or sometimes tax on sale of
property if it is sold within a number of years after
buying it. Be aware and careful of taxes as they
could seriously erode any upside potential to your
property investment.

◆ Commission: This varies between 1% and 3% in
most countries. In most cases, it is paid by the
seller, or shared between buyer and seller. In
countries like China, it is typically paid entirely by
the buyer. Advertising a property through online
property portals is increasingly popular, and this
typically involves lower commission too, so this
may be a worthwhile avenue to explore, especially
if you have to pay the commission.

◆ Legal Fee: Beside stamp duty and commission,
a legal fee is also unavoidable in any property
transaction. Depending on the complexity of
the transaction, the fee could range from a few
thousand dollars to about 1% of the transaction
value. In some jurisdictions, the mortgage
bank might help with recommending you a
conveyancing lawyer and even help subsidise some
of the legal costs if you take up the mortgage with
them.

◆ Neighbours: Be careful of bad neighbourhoods
and bad neighbours. This is sometimes easily
forgotten as one is usually too focused on the
property in question. It is worthwhile paying the

neighbours a visit. Speak with them to understand the neighbourhood, understand the history of the property you are interested in, and have a feel of whether they are likely to be "neighbours from hell". In most instances you would be fine with your neighbours, but it is worthwhile finding out who your neighbours might be before you buy. If nothing else, sometimes just speaking with them on the property you intend to buy may uncover interesting facts that could affect your decision.

Buying a Foreign Property

If you have decided that the best investment property to buy is one in a foreign country, then there are a few more points you should not ignore. Besides the points raised earlier on location, taxes and commissions, a key factor often not considered is foreign exchange or FX exposure. This is probably one of the most important considerations for foreign property purchases, as very often what you make from property price appreciation may be completely wiped out by currency depreciation!

You can't completely avoid the FX risk in any foreign investment, but you could try to hedge or minimise the risk. For a foreign property purchase, consider how much you would like to finance your property and also in what currency. Assuming you converted from your home currency into foreign currency for the first 30% down-payment and you are taking a mortgage for 70% of the property, you have one big decision to make – to finance in the foreign currency or in your home currency?

(a) Financing in the Foreign Currency

This is the more common route. In this case, you do not lock in the FX rate for the 70% mortgage, and you are expected to buy the foreign currency every month at the going FX rate for the mortgage repayment. Assuming you have rental income in the foreign currency, then the rent would partly offset the mortgage repayment in most cases, resulting in a much smaller FX purchase required every month.

- ❖ **Pros:** You would benefit from a falling FX rate as you would be able to buy your FX cheaper to service the mortgage.

- ❖ **Cons:** You will pay more if FX rate goes up.

Now consider what happens when you sell the property. The sale proceeds in foreign currency would be used to pay down the outstanding mortgage which is also denominated in the foreign currency, so there is no currency mismatch. The balance would be equivalent to your 30% paid, plus whatever principal you have repaid all these years, plus any capital gains in the foreign currency. You will then convert the foreign currency into your home currency. If the FX value had gone up, you would make more from your investment, and vice versa.

(b) Financing in your Home Currency

Banks in your home country sometimes offer mortgage loans for foreign properties. When they do, you would typically lock in the entire mortgage amount in your home currency using the FX rate at the point of mortgage drawdown. You would then service your loan in local currency going forward.

- ◈ **Pros:** You are free from FX conversion every month to service your mortgage, and not subjected to FX movements.

- ◈ **Cons:** You get your rental income in the foreign currency, and you may have little use for it unless you convert it back to your home currency periodically, which then subjects you to FX volatility.

Now when you sell your property, you would have to repay your mortgage in your home currency. However, given the sale proceeds would be in foreign currency, you would have to do a one-time conversion for the entire proceeds into your home currency, repay the outstanding mortgage, and the balance will be your share. If the FX rate had gone up, you would make more money as your entire proceeds would stand to gain from this FX appreciation. If the FX had gone down, you would expose the entire sale proceeds to this FX risk, which could potentially eat into your 30% down-payment, resulting in capital loss.

The math is clear for the two financing methods. Here are your options:

- ◈ If you are bullish on the FX rate for the long run, you would be better off financing it now in your home currency.

◆ If you are bearish on the FX rate, you should be financing it in the foreign currency, and also hedging the 30% that you put down.

◆ If you do not have a view of the underlying FX rate, you would be better off financing it in the foreign currency, and either hedging or leaving the 30% unhedged.

Let me summarise it in a table for easy reference:

	Finance in your **home currency**	Finance in the **foreign currency**	**FX hedge?**
You think the foreign currency will **appreciate**	✔		No need if you are confident of your view, or hedge when your view changes
You have **no view** on the foreign currency		✔	Optional, for part of the capital paid
You think the foreign currency will **depreciate**		✔	Yes, hedge your capital paid against a fall of the foreign currency

In the scenario where you don't have an FX view, leaving your 30% down-payment and subsequent principal repayment unhedged means you will leave it to chance what the FX rate may be when you sell your property.

Let's look at a numerical example:

On Day 1, you bought a A$1 million house in
Australia. Your home currency is Singapore Dollars.
AUD/SGD FX is 1.30. You borrowed 70% in AUD,
and paid A$300,000 cash by converting S$390,000.

Over the next five years, assume your rental paid
for the interest of the mortgage exactly, and your
monthly mortgage repayment resulted in you repaying say A$100,000 of the principal owed. Assume
further you were in a falling AUD environment, and
your average FX rate where you paid down this 10%
of purchase price was at 1.15, you would have paid
another S$115,000.

On the first day of the sixth year, you sold your house
at a price net of all costs of A$1.2 million. AUD/SGD
was at 1.00 then. You repaid your outstanding loan of
A$600,000, and were left with A$600,000, as compared to your total paid of S$505,000, so you made a
total return of S$95,000 over the five years, or about
19% of your paid up.

For comparison purposes, if AUD/SGD had not
fallen and was back at 1.30 instead of 1.00, your gains
in SGD terms would have been ($600,000 × 1.3 –
$505,000 =) S$275,000 or 54%.

The above example is one of leaving the initial capital unhedged. As you can see, your gains were reduced, no thanks

to adverse FX movements, by (\$275k – \$95k =) S\$180,000. If you had put on a hedge against a falling AUD, say by holding a short AUD position or through other derivatives like FX options, you would probably have saved a good part of this S\$180,000. Conversely, if you had put on the hedge and the AUD/SGD had appreciated instead, you would not have been able to participate in most of the upside of the AUD too.

Now if you had financed the mortgage in SGD because you were bullish AUD/SGD, you would have been wrong, and this is how much you would have ended up with:

At the then AUD/SGD rate of 1.30, you locked in your AUD borrowing of A\$700,000 in Singapore dollars, i.e. S\$910,000. For simplicity, assume you repaid 10% of the original purchase price, i.e. S\$130,000 over the next five years.

Now if you sold your house at A\$1.2 million, at FX rate of 1.00 you would have S\$1.2 million too. After repaying the mortgage outstanding of S\$780,000, you would now be left with S\$420,000. Compared to the total you paid of (S\$390,000 + 130,000 =) S\$520,000, you would have lost S\$100,000!

This example illustrates how important FX is in foreign real estate investments. The capital gains can be completely wiped out and more if FX moves against you. The choice of financing currency could mitigate part of this risk. So if one does not want to take a bet on the currency movements, it is crucial to pick the right financing currencies and consider putting a hedge on the capital.

When Should You Sell?

We have gone through extensively the factors affecting real estate prices, and our focus has largely been on buying it. As with most investments, buying it might be the easy part. When should one sell, especially for an asset that comes with large transaction costs? It is easy to say you should sell when prices have topped out, just like recommending one to buy when prices have bottomed out. But do we know when the trend has turned for sure? Just as in observing market trends before buying, one should closely observe market trends after buying too. In my view, there are a few triggers for thinking about selling:

- ◆ When you have held on to the property for many years and seen prices run up, resulting in property prices being a little unaffordable for the young.

- ◆ When you see the country's economy turning down structurally, and it is not expected to turn up anytime soon.

- ◆ When you see opportunity that is unique to your property, e.g. if a developer offers above market prices for redevelopment.

- ◆ When interest rates start to inch up significantly, but it is not so much related to the country's economy turning better as it is to other reasons like being linked to a rise in global interest rates.

- When the supply outstrips the demand by a huge margin over the next few years.

- When the rental yield falls so much that it does not even cover the interest portion of your mortgage, or when you could not rent it out after trying for many months!

Just as it is almost impossible to be buying at the low, it is also very difficult to sell at the top. If you follow the above triggers, and you see a few of them coming true, it would be time to consider taking profit on your property. Remember it is not easy to sell an illiquid asset like real estate. Sometimes it takes many months or even over a year to sell, so waiting for the absolute top before marketing your property for sale may already be too late, especially if the market starts to turn down quickly after the peak.

Conclusion

Real estate may be the single largest investment one makes. It is sometimes scary to pull the trigger to make the purchase. This chapter has described the factors one should consider before making the decision, and some key ones include location, physical attributes and price. It is of crucial importance to do sufficient research and due diligence before buying, as any wrong decision is costly to unwind, due to the illiquid nature of real estate and the high transaction costs.

As an investment asset, one could consider foreign property too, but that requires even more consideration, especially the impact of foreign exchange. Having the right financing and hedging strategy goes a long way in mitigating the risk of FX eroding your capital gains.

Once you have bought your property, it is equally important to know the right time to sell. A list of triggers could be considered and if a few of them are satisfied, it may be time to take profit.

CHAPTER 3

Foreign Exchange

FOREIGN EXCHANGE, or FX for short, is the conversion of one country's currency into another. The rate at which the exchange is conducted is simply called the Exchange Rate, or FX Rate. One can think of exchange rates as basically the price of one country's currency in another currency. FX is the largest traded instrument in the world, and it is growing at an explosive pace. According to the BIS Triennial Central Bank Survey, trading in foreign exchange markets averaged $5.3 trillion per day in April 2013. This was up from $4.0 trillion in April 2010 and $3.3 trillion in April 2007. To have a sense of the scale, FX turnover in one day is more than the annual GDP of Japan, the world's fourth largest economy!

Trading is increasingly concentrated in the largest financial centres of the world. In April 2013, sales desks in the UK, the USA, Singapore and Japan intermediated 71% of FX trading, compared to 66% in April 2010. With this kind of turnover, FX is here to stay and cannot be ignored. FX affects almost everything we do on a daily basis, directly or indirectly, especially in our investments which are increasingly global. So, whether we trade FX or not, it is important to understand FX, especially its impact on the rest of our portfolio investments.

To cover FX in its entirety would require an entire book, not just a chapter. Here I will not attempt to go through everything about FX in depth, but just cover the essential points to give retail investors sufficient information to understand FX and consider whether FX is an investment instrument you want to be involved in.

FX Basics

Foreign exchange is not a difficult instrument to understand. However, the man on the street sometimes struggles to understand it simply because of the naming convention. For example, does "USD/JPY spot rate at 120" mean the price of USD or the price of JPY, and what exactly is it denominated in? Let's go through some of the basic concepts of FX.

- ◆ FX Spot: This simply means the settlement cycle of the FX transaction is two business days. Anything more than two business days would be called FX Forward, and is covered in the derivatives section. In trading jargon, if investors buy an FX pair, they will say they are "long" the currency pair. If they sell it, they will be "short" the currency pair.

- ◆ Base Currency and Term Currency: Base currency is the first currency in a currency pair, while the second currency is called the Term currency. Exchange rates are quoted in per unit of the base currency. The Euro is the dominant base currency against all other global currencies. All currency pairs traded against the Euro are quoted per €1. The hierarchy for the major currencies is as follows: EUR, GBP, AUD, NZD, USD, CAD, CHF, JPY. For example, the market convention to quote the exchange rate between the Australian Dollar and the Japanese Yen would be AUD/JPY, i.e. how many Yen is A$1 worth. Similarly, EUR/USD rate of 1.10 would mean €1 is worth US$1.10.

❖ Bid and Offer: In most other instruments like stocks, investors have no problem knowing which price applies when buying or selling. In FX, people can be confused because it involves two currencies, and many do not know what it means. An easy way to think about it is that a buyer has to pay more for the currency, while a seller receives less. For example, if USD/JPY is quoted at 120.45–120.50, the buyer of USD will pay ¥120.50, i.e. more JPY per USD, while the seller of USD will receive ¥120.45.

What Drives FX Movements?

There are many types of participants involved in FX every day. They can be corporate, banks, tourists, government bodies, traders, investors, speculators, etc. But as mentioned at the start, FX is an incredibly big market, and it is driven largely by professional traders. Real trade-related FX accounts for an extremely small portion of the daily turnover.

For the professional traders, they are broadly divided into two camps:

(a) Fundamental-Driven

It is easy to say what the fundamentals are for a stock, as one could easily quantify the sales revenue, profitability, growth potential, etc., for a company. What then are fundamentals for the currency of a country? They encompass practically everything that affects the country, as anything that affects the country would affect at least the demand for the currency, and sometimes also the supply.

Some of the more common "fundamentals" that FX traders look at include:

- Economic policies and conditions – e.g. employment, GDP, inflation, trade, current account.

- Central bank policies and interventions – e.g. fixing, competitive devaluation, interest rate and/ or FX mandate.

- Politics – e.g. government policies, central bank policies, relationships with neighbouring countries, political stability.

- Corporate and other actions – e.g. mergers and acquisitions, repatriation, debt or equity issuance, stock and bond market performances.

Broadly speaking, what is good for a country is good for the currency. For example, a country experiencing robust GDP growth would typically have high and increasing domestic interest rates. Fundamental traders attracted to it would put on the popular "carry trade" – buying a currency with a higher interest rate and selling a currency with a lower rate. Conversely, a country experiencing political instability would usually see their currency being sold, in favour of another country/currency with a more stable political environment.

Other than the fundamentals of a country, FX rates are also affected frequently by changes in the demand and supply of the underlying currencies. For example, a large Merger and Acquisition deal where a company in Country A is buying a company in Country B would normally be short-term positive for the currency of Country B, and negative for the currency of Country A. It is worth bearing in mind that FX is the relative value of one currency to another. This implies that knowing just the fundamental of one currency alone is not sufficient. It is always the relative strength or weakness of two currencies that results in movements in FX.

Fundamentals do not usually see big changes all that frequently, so what most traders pay attention to is the change at the margin to these fundamentals, or sometimes the change to the expectations of these fundamentals. Not all fundamental factors are important at all times. For example, inflation may not be in focus when we operate in a low-inflation environment for a long time and the country is bugged by other more pressing issues. It is thus important to keep tabs on fundamental issues, and in particular know what is in focus, or even better, be one step ahead of other investors in knowing what will be the focus.

(b) Technical-Driven

"Technical" typically refers to chart patterns. This may include not just price charts but also charts on underlying fundamentals or practically anything remotely linked to the country or currency, in order to predict the price trend of the currency. There are many types of technical traders: they could be Short-term or Long-term, Trend-following versus Mean Reversion, or a combination. They could also be trading based on modelling human behaviour, generally called Behavioural Finance. Or they could be the increasingly popular High Frequency Traders, which buy and sell in nanoseconds, based on technical or other people's actions.

Technical traders in general believe that all the information, including fundamentals, is out there in the market and is reflected in the price. For them, there is little value in analysing fundamentals; the value lies in analysing how market participants would likely react to a certain price level or trend.

Derivatives of FX

A derivative is something which derives its value from an underlying asset or assets. In the case of FX, the following are all considered FX derivatives:

(a) FX Forwards

This is an FX contract where the exchange of one currency against another is agreed for a future date and at a pre-agreed rate today. FX Forwards are almost a "plain vanilla" product nowadays, and many trade it like FX Spot. The key difference is that one does not need to "roll" the trade so frequently like an FX Spot because the first maturity date is at a future date.

The most important concept for an FX Forward is that the forward price generally reflects the "no arbitrage" price due to the difference in the interest rates of the two currencies. In an efficient market, the "forward point", or the difference between the forward price and the spot price, is just the difference in the interest rates expressed in FX terms. What it means is that a currency with higher interest rate is expected to depreciate in the future. The opposite is true too, i.e. a currency with lower interest rate would be priced to appreciate in the FX Forward pricing. The reason is that one has to be compensated for holding on to a lower-yielding currency, and the reward is a higher FX Forward price, and vice versa. If the FX Forward market is not priced as such, an arbitrageur could in theory buy the higher-yielding currency now and invest in an interest-yielding instrument, financed by borrowing the lower-yielding currency, and at the same time enter into an FX Forward trade to sell the high-yielding currency to lock in an almost risk-free return. These arbitrage activities will force either the rates or the forward points to adjust to a no-arbitrage point.

The above breaks down when there is restriction of free market flow of capital or during periods of heavy market speculation or market dislocation. For example, the USD/ CNH (Chinese Renminbi traded offshore) forward was priced for a stronger CNH in most of the period prior to 2015 even though the CNH was yielding higher than USD. That was when speculation for CNH to appreciate was rampant, and the market was selling USD/CNH forwards (and swaps) irrespective of what the forward points implied.

(b) Non-Deliverable Forwards or NDFs

This is similar to an FX Forward except that there is no exchange of currencies at the forward date. Instead, the difference between the contracted FX rate and the FX spot rate on maturity is net-settled on the delivery date in the base currency, which is usually USD. A fixing methodology is agreed when the NDF deal is contracted specifying a pre-determined source as a reference on the maturity or fixing date. NDFs only exist typically for emerging countries whose currencies are controlled domestically, for example the Chinese Renminbi or Yuan. To circumvent those controls, traders created NDFs to trade these currencies, and since they are only traded outside the home countries, they fall outside the purview of the home countries.

Here is a quick comparison between Deliverable FX Forwards and NDFs:

Deliverable Forwards	Non-Deliverable Forwards
Conducted in the home country where exchange of currencies is permitted on the settlement date	Conducted in an offshore country where exchange of currencies is not permitted on the settlement date
Gains or losses are not cash settled	On the settlement date, the forward is marked-to-market. The resulting cash gain or loss is received or paid. Settlement is against a pre-agreed fixing benchmark
No basis risk, just deliver on settlement date	Basis risk exists as there is a gap between the benchmark rate and final spot conversion rate

(c) FX Swaps

This is an FX Spot and an FX Forward combined. Essentially, the parties of an FX Swap agree to exchange the currencies at the beginning, and exchange it back at the forward date. According to BIS Survey 2013, FX Swaps were the most actively traded instruments in April 2013, at $2.2 trillion per day, ahead of FX Spot trading at $2.0 trillion. An FX Swap can be used as a short-term funding instrument as basically one is borrowing a currency for a period and promising right from the outset to return the currency at a future date. This is useful when a corporate or a bank has currency mismatch, i.e. too much of one currency but short of another currency. FX Swap is also used to roll or extend an FX position to a further out date. The "swap point", which is the cost to do the FX Swap, is in most cases just the interest rate differential between the two currencies expressed in FX points.

(d) FX Options

An FX Option gives the owner of the option the right but not the obligation to buy or sell FX at or any time up to a certain maturity date at a pre-agreed rate. As the owner has the option to "exercise" his rights, he would naturally have to pay for this right. This is a derivative that is leveraged but at the same time will not lose the buyer of the option much money other than the price of the option. On the other hand, the seller of the option will receive a "premium" for selling it, and is exposed to unlimited risks just like an FX Forward.

As with all other options, the most common vanilla options are Calls and Puts. Unlike other options like stock options, there are two currencies in an FX, so the investor must be clear which direction the option is betting for. For example, a bet for a higher USD/JPY is called USD Call JPY Put, or some simply call USD/JPY Call. The latter assumes one knows the naming convention well, so to avoid ambiguity I prefer the former.

When one buys or sells an option, one is really making a call on the underlying volatility. If you think the underlying currency pair is likely to trade in a more volatile fashion going forward, one way to express the view is to buy a call or a put option. You could also sell an option if your view is that a currency pair is likely to calm down and trade in a more orderly manner going forward.

More exotic option types include Knock-Out or Knock-In options, One-Touch or No-Touch options, or a combination of them. The risk and reward profiles for these exotic options are more complicated, so only dabble in them if you are absolutely sure what you are getting yourself into.

(e) FX Futures

These are contracts typically traded on exchanges with standard sizes per contract and with fixed delivery dates in the future. These contracts function just like FX Forwards, except there is a fixed structure to them. FX Futures are making inroads slowly into the FX market, which is still dominated traditionally by over-the-counter inter-bank business. Unless investors and traders change their long-term habits, FX Futures are likely to continue to play only a supporting role in the overall FX market.

What Should I Consider Before Trading in FX?

Most people seem to have a view on FX. They probably get the view from newspapers or research reports or from listening to others. FX is also easy to get involved in, as it needs little capital, and many trading or broking houses or banks are willing to lend many times your capital for you to trade. To me, FX is a simple-to-understand instrument, but an extremely difficult instrument to master. There are several reasons for this.

The main reason is that too many factors drive FX movements, and what worked yesterday may not work today. For example, if the US Non-Farm Payroll (NFP) number released on the first Friday of every month turns out to be stronger than the market expects, should one buy or sell USD? In most cases, the answer is probably an unambiguous *buy*. However there are times when a higher-than-expected NFP leads market participants to think that the US Federal Reserve is going to hike rates more aggressively, leading to an equity market selloff, and drag the USD down in the process. This is just one example; there are numerous others.

Another reason is that there are too many participants in the FX market and the market is simply too efficient. With a daily turnover of over $5 trillion, there is a large number of participants trading unbelievable amounts every second of the trading week, from 5am New Zealand time on Monday to 6pm US time on Friday. Many of them are professional traders for banks or funds. There are also many funds with machines trading the market with little human intervention, which are able to react to market data releases or developments faster than a human could. What are the chances of success for retail investors? In my view, a retail investor will always lose out in the long run if he is trading for the short term, as he will always be slower than a professional trader or machine. Where a retail investor has an edge is the ability to have longer-term views, and the willingness and ability to sit out the volatility without the need to report trading performances on a monthly basis like a fund. This requires the retail investor not to have high leverage, as that would limit his ability to sit out the volatility. That does not mean sitting on a position doing nothing and waiting for the position to come in one's favour either. Money management skills are still required, and that includes cutting a position when it turns bad, and taking profit when necessary.

Two pieces of trading advice I could give for all potential retail FX investors/traders/speculators:

◈ Plan your stop loss level *before* you enter the trade. Having a profit taking level in mind as well is also good discipline. When the market trades towards one's stop loss or profit taking level, most people are tempted to move the level further away. I advise against that unless there is new information available that necessitates re-evaluation.

◈ Continuously evaluate a position you have by asking if your reason for being in the trade is still there. If and when the reason for having the position is no longer there, or the risk/reward ratio is no longer compelling, get out!

The above pointers are good for trading any asset class, but are especially important for FX investors because of the speed at which FX moves and the leverage that one has. Investors have very little time to stop and think, so it is crucial to have a game plan ready and execute it when the time comes. "Cut first, talk later" is often heard when a stop loss level is reached. That makes a lot of sense due to the volatile nature of the FX market. Many times, you will feel stupid for cutting a position and see the market reverse immediately in your face. But trust me, the one time that the market does not come back after you cut your position is going to save you more money than you would ever make had you not cut your positions in the past.

Transaction costs for FX are relatively small, probably the smallest among all financial instruments. Do not feel sorry for getting out of a losing position. Once you are out of a position, you will find that you can think a lot clearer. If at that point in time you still think that you should get back into the position, you could do so with a well-considered point of view. Don't forget to set new stop loss and profit taking levels.

Another important consideration before you rush out to trade FX is how much leverage to trade with. Usually trading portals or banks give you about 5 times to 20 times leverage, and it becomes tempting to trade more than you should. Remember that it is very easy to lose *all* the money you have and more, due to leverage, when the market moves against you. The mathematics is rather simple. If you are leveraged 20 times, a 5% move against you will wipe out all your capital. While a 5% move isn't likely or common in a day or two, one should know that over a period of a week or a month it is absolutely plausible.

In January 2015, we saw that when the Swiss National Bank (SNB) gave up with its Euro/Swiss Franc (EUR/CHF) support, the EUR/CHF fell from 1.20 to below 1.05 in seconds. That is a magnitude of more than 12.5%, pretty much unheard of for developed market currencies.

EUR/CHF price chart on 15 January 2015

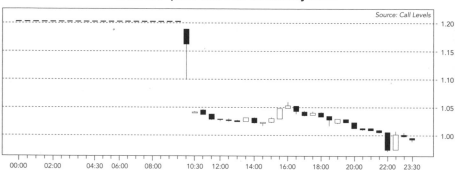

Stop loss orders left in the market at just below 1.20 were executed at much lower level, mostly at below 1.05, causing huge losses to everyone with a long EUR/CHF position. As EUR/CHF was a very stable currency pair prior to that fateful day, most investors who traded that currency pair had large positions on. They had been buying EUR/CHF just above 1.20 and selling it slightly higher, between 1.21 and 1.25, for the last few years prior to that day. They were successful playing this strategy for the longest time, leaning on SNB's support, so much so that they increased their leverage over time to take advantage of small moves in the EUR/CHF. As such, when EUR/CHF fell through the support, everyone was scrambling to get out of a very narrow door, magnifying the move in a very short period of time.

In numbers, if a retail investor had €100,000 in his trading account, and he used all of it to buy EUR/CHF at 10 times

EUR/CHF price chart since March 2012

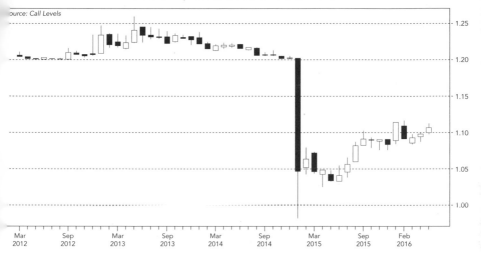

Source: Call Levels

leverage, he would have had a long €1,000,000 and short CHF1,200,000 position. On the day EUR/CHF collapsed, if he managed to cut his position at 1.00, he would have lost CHF200,000, or €200,000 at the then EUR/CHF price of 1.00. That would have required him to top up €100,000 immediately to cover his losses, or face claims or lawsuits from the shop that extended him the credit line!

Thankfully, an event like the above does not happen that often. We can't really plan for it, but at the same time we need to put in place safeguards to ensure that our entire portfolio is not wiped out in one black swan event like that. To do so, leveraged FX trading should not constitute a large part of a person's portfolio. If one limits FX trading to no more than say 5–10% of one's wealth, and limits leverage to 10x, even if an event like the EUR/CHF were to happen again, one would not be wiped out completely. One should size the portfolio according to the volatility of the underlying currency pair and one's risk appetite. Remember that the trading shops give you a lot of rope (aka limit) to hang yourself. It is you who must exercise self-control and remember not to over-leverage.

FX as a Hedging Tool

We have established that FX is a highly leveraged and sometimes volatile instrument. Even if we are not involved in directly trading it, we need to understand it better as it impacts almost every aspect of our life and especially our investment portfolio. If we have overseas assets or investment products denominated in non-home currency, then the impact is going to be even more direct. For example, if we buy US stocks and our home base is Singapore, then we need to consider the impact of USD/SGD FX on our overall return. If we are not careful, the gains from the stocks could be completely wiped out by FX moves.

A case can be made to use FX as a hedge instead of as a trading instrument. Most retail investors do not like the real meaning of a "hedge", as that means it only pays out when the instrument you are hedging against goes against you, and vice versa. So they find little joy in "losing less". Thus, most people engage in FX as an outright trading tool, hoping to make some money in the near term to supplement their portfolio returns. For example, in an environment of a rising USD against the UK Sterling Pounds (GBP), even if the non-UK based investor has a property in UK, he may just trade GBP/USD sporadically independent of his exposure in the UK, instead of hedging against a falling GBP.

The argument for not hedging a currency move is usually that currency moves in large cycles, or "what moves up must come down". Hedging costs money too, so by doing nothing, one saves if the currency does come back to the starting level over time. While that may be true of some currencies over selected periods of time, it can also be extremely costly if it turns out otherwise. A good example is GBP/USD, which hasn't come back to its starting level over time.

GBP/USD 10-year chart

The key difference between calling an FX trade a "hedge" and an "investment" is probably the frequency the trade is put on and taken off. A hedge is usually put on for the medium term, to guard against a fall of a currency. An investment or trade is usually done more frequently, trading in and out when the market moves. Some who trade their "hedges" in and out call it an "active hedge", to improve the returns and hedge against a falling currency at the same time. That usually means one would remove a hedge when the hedge moves in one's favour too much too fast for example, and put it back on when the currency pair retraces. It really does not matter what you call it, as long as you are clear in your mind what you are doing it for, and are prepared to face the consequences if you are wrong.

Personally, I feel that a retail investor trading FX from the starting point of it being a hedge has merits. If nothing else it gives some comfort to the investor if the FX trade or hedge goes against him, since he knows then that his underlying investment he is hedging against is going in his favour. At the same time, this investor should not be in a hurry to take his profit if the FX hedge goes in his favour, otherwise his risk-reward would be wrongly skewed! Contrast that with the scenario in which he starts with trading the opposite side of the hedge; he would probably be totally stressed if the trade goes against him, as it is "double whammy" for him, losing in both. Therefore, if done in a smart way, one could in theory help offset the potential FX losses from the underlying foreign investments and potentially add some value to one's portfolio.

Is FX Really Equivalent to Cash?

FX is a very liquid product and can be converted from one currency to another in a maximum of two working days. When a retail investor considers how liquid to be, he usually just thinks in terms of how much cash in base currency to be placed in deposit products, or at most a highly liquid money market instrument. As FX is quite like cash, it frequently features in investors' minds. However, a retail investor normally does not expect to lose any money in cash or deposit products, but there is a distinct possibility of losing money doing FX when converted to one's home currency. As such, FX should ideally not be thought of as "cash" unless the investor has real underlying needs in that foreign currency and does not mind having some cash in a currency other than his home currency.

If an investor has no underlying foreign currency need and does not mind risking part of his cash holdings to make more, then the investor must be very clear how much he is willing to risk and possibly lose, as mentioned in the earlier paragraphs on how to size an FX portfolio. It is not advisable to risk everything in the cash holdings, as cash is there to provide stability to a person's liquidity needs. FX is an extremely efficient instrument widely participated in by experts globally. It is difficult enough for the professionals to consistently add value over time, retail investors must really have a unique edge to be able to outperform them and make money over time.

Conclusion

Foreign exchange is the largest traded instrument in the world. It is efficient and exciting at the same time. In reality, the volatility in FX is a lot smaller than individual stocks, but the perception is that it is more volatile probably because traders are usually leveraged several times in FX, as opposed to the normally unleveraged trading in stocks. So a seemingly small move in FX could make or lose the trader a lot of money, creating the impression that it is "volatile". It is also because of this easy access to leverage that makes FX a very exciting and "sexy" instrument to trade.

Detractors liken FX to a "casino", as the moves in FX appear random to them. Proponents think it is possible to add value in FX as they are able to detect order in the perceived chaos of the FX market. There are also many non-profit-motivated players in the form of governments, tourists, etc., who provide the opportunities for professionals to take advantage of.

Whatever one's belief may be, it is clear that FX cannot be ignored, as it impacts our daily life. Understanding FX and how we could use it to our advantage, be it for trading or hedging purposes, would be the smart way to go. If used wisely, FX could be another source of "alpha" or value-add. The downside of FX could also be detrimental due to the high leverage typically employed. As such, the key is really to limit FX to a small part of one's portfolio, limit the leverage, and consider using it largely as a hedge against the underlying FX exposures of one's other assets.

CHAPTER 4

Other Asset Classes

BESIDES THE three common main asset classes of Equities, Fixed Income and Cash/Cash Equivalents, and the popular Real Estate and Foreign Exchange, there are a few other asset classes used sparingly by more sophisticated retail investors and High Net Worth Individuals. They are Commodities, Private Equity and Hedge Funds. We will take a look at each of these in this chapter, to see how they can allow you to pick up more yield and diversify your wealth.

COMMODITIES

Commodities here refers to raw materials or primary products that are of value and traded across borders. These commodities are produced in large quantities and are fungible (interchangeable) because they are of uniform quality even though they are produced by many different producers. For the purpose of this chapter, we refer only to commodities

79

traded on commodities exchanges. The most common commodities exchanges in the world include:

◆ New York Mercantile Exchange (NYMEX)

◆ London Metal Exchange (LME)

◆ Chicago Board of Trade (CBOT)

◆ Chicago Mercantile Exchange (CME)

There are also many commodities exchanges in China, given that it has probably been the biggest consumer of commodities in recent years. These exchanges are spread out over several cities and trade their own commodities contracts which are of relevance to their own state/province. The most popular commodities exchanges in China are probably the Shanghai Futures Exchange and the Shanghai Gold Exchange.

In the early 2010s, post global financial crisis, commodities gained in popularity as an asset class among global investors. That may have been partially due to the fall in USD, which is the de facto currency of choice when pricing commodities. The fall in USD partly led to an increase in global commodities prices, which led to even more investors keen to use commodities as a diversifier or a hedge against price falls in other asset classes.

Many things can come under the "Commodities" banner. For the purpose of investment, the common types are Gold, Oil, Grains and Metals (more generically, Precious Metals, Energy, Agriculture, and Base Metals, respectively). Within each type are numerous different contracts, of different quality, grade, contract size, delivery location, etc. There are specialised traders in each of the commodities sub-classes, and they live and breathe the commodity, knowing everything about the demand and supply data for them. The more sophisticated even look at related data to forecast future changes in demand and supply. For example, orange juice traders may be tracking the weather data to forecast potential changes to the coming harvest. Copper traders may be dissecting the import and export data of copper from and to China to decipher how much is due to real needs and how much is due to financial engineering.

By now you will probably have some appreciation that commodities constitute a big and complex asset class that cuts across so many things that we can't possibly be familiar with all of them. Data affecting these commodities is not as easily available as for stocks, for example. If one wants to be trading in commodities, one would be at a huge disadvantage compared to professional traders, unless one is already in or familiar with that particular type of commodities trade business. In my view, a retail investor trading an unfamiliar commodity as an investment is no different from gambling, as he would have less than 50% chance of making money in this complex trading world largely dominated by profession-als. As such, I will not be advocating a retail investor or even HNWI to be involved much in commodities trading or hedg-ing. If one really insists on trading commodities or using it as a hedge, I would recommend only the most commonly traded financial commodity – gold.

To a great extent, gold is probably more a "currency" than a commodity. The supply of gold in the world is known to a large extent, while the demand for it is mostly due to financial demands rather than industrial needs, unlike other precious or base metals. Jewellery demand by retail investors obviously does affect the demand and therefore prices, but recent years have seen financial instruments like Gold ETFs taking over as the main drivers of gold price changes. Gold is also treated more like a currency than a commodity in most banks, with "paper gold" easily traded without taking delivery of the physical gold. Once the physical aspect of gold is side-stepped, gold can then be traded just like other currencies via a debit and credit of gold in the account balance.

Valuing Commodities

Think of commodities as goods that you could buy in a super-market. A commodity, or any good, is worth as much as what a marginal buyer is willing to pay for it. Apologies for stating the obvious, but price falls when supply exceeds demand, and vice versa. Obviously there are numerous factors that affect the demand and supply of any commodity. Understanding these factors is crucial to being able to appreciate if current prices are cheap or expensive.

However, unlike valuing a bond or a stock, one cannot really confidently state a "fair" price for most commodities as there are no cash flows to discount in commodities. Most analysts would base valuation off a commodity's historical prices instead, and adjust it by inflation or cost of living, etc. We cannot generalise how to value commodities, as each commodity has its own unique characteristics and factors affecting its demand and supply. Let's examine the case of gold, and one should hopefully be able to infer from that how to value other commodities.

In the case of gold, even though most investors treat gold like a currency, it does not have its own "country fundamentals" as it is not owned or manufactured by any single country. So valuing gold involves studying closely the factors affecting its demand and supply. Here are some factors affecting the demand and supply of gold:

- Gold production/mining

- Jewellers' physical/investment gold demand

- End consumers' jewellery demand

- Gold ETF demand

- Central Bank gold reserves accumulation/divesting

- Financial investors/hedgers' demand

Gold's new supply is generally known, and it largely comes from gold mines. This production number is largely quantifiable as there is a limited supply of gold underground on Earth.

The biggest unknown for supply comes from the largest holders of gold – the central banks of the world. In the nine years between 1996 and 2004, when gold hovered between $250 and $400 an ounce, there was very little interest in gold. Central banks were seen selling gold on the quiet from their reserves, as gold was then seen as a questionable store of wealth for nations. When gold prices started to rally above $400 from 2004 to a high of almost $1890 per ounce in 2011, the central banks' selling stopped, and in fact some buying was noted, as gold again become an acceptable store of wealth, especially in the face of falling USD. Central banks sometimes report their gold holdings, but this is after long time lags, so timely information of supply from central banks is usually not available.

Demand for gold is more seasonal and cyclical. When gold was trading at $400, retail investors never talked about gold as an investment asset. Once gold was rallying quickly above $500 from the end of 2005, investors started to take notice and began to pile in. Interest in gold ETFs jumped in multiples, propelled by professional and retail investors alike. At the height of the craze in 2011, talk of gold hitting $2000 or even $3000 was rife. Central banks were also seen net accumulating gold during this period. This resulted in retail investors buying everything gold, like gold nuggets, gold bars and gold jewellery. This phenomenon was especially clear in China, where the gold jewellers were doing roaring business not just onshore, but also in Hong Kong. China quickly became the world's biggest consumer of gold around then, overtaking India. And since then, China and India have been competing neck and neck for that title. When the gold rally ended and gold traded below $1400 from mid-2013, so did the retail euphoria. With gold trading between $1100 and $1200 for most of 2015, the "buy on rally" type of retail gold investing became a thing of the past. The gold market is arguably more balanced nowadays, with less speculative interest but more real or hedging investors.

With prices holding above $1200 at the time of writing, is that the "fair price" for gold? Forecasts from banks and gold experts are forecasting future gold prices between $1100 and

$1400, much more within reason compared to 2011. Many of these forecasts are based on studies of underlying demand and supply, while some of them are based on technical forecasts. Whatever they are based on, I dare say that not many experts have got it right consistently over the last 20 years. This just demonstrates that even the experts struggle to get it right, let alone a retail investor who has far less access to the information that is available to these professional researchers and investors.

Investing in Commodities

For retail investors, dealing with physical commodities is a non-starter. That leaves only "paper" trading or commodities futures trading (without delivery). As commodities contracts have different unique features, depending on which exchange they are trading on, investors must be extremely careful before dipping their toes in.

Trading in commodities futures is similar to trading stock futures. Both are done on a leverage basis, and involve buying or selling a contract for delivery on a future date. As taking delivery of commodities is certainly not a retail investor's objective, one should take extra care to close the position before maturity, roll it over to a longer future date, or cash settle it.

Specifically for gold, retail investors can gain exposure via several means:

❖ Buying gold (bars) from gold jewellers or banks

❖ Through a paper gold account in a bank

- ◈ Buying/selling gold through a trading account

- ◈ Buying/selling gold futures

Buying physical gold is what most investors could do. One should be aware, however, that buying gold jewellery incurs a huge premium over the prevailing gold price due to the additional costs of designing and making the gold jewellery. Buying gold-bar-like pendants, of weights from say 2g to 20g, is similar to buying gold jewellery, but perhaps with slightly less premium due to the simplicity of design. Buying investment gold bars of above 20g is the preferred method of physical gold investing as they are not ornamental in nature, and typically come with a fixed bid-ask spread, i.e. the bank or jewellery shop would promise to buy back at a certain fixed spread at the then prevailing gold price.

Investing through a paper gold account is the simplest non-physical way of investing in gold, but involves probably the largest bid-ask spread of paper gold trading, though it is still much smaller than retail physical gold buying. This method is good for a long-term investor who is inactive in trading, and merely wants to buy and hold gold as an alternative asset class. For the investor who wants to trade gold actively, opening a trading account to either trade gold spot or forward or futures would be the way to go. The risk here is the high leverage available, and therefore only the most sophisticated investors should dabble in this, due to the extreme volatility in gold prices.

PRIVATE EQUITY

Private Equity (PE) refers to companies that are not publicly listed on any exchanges. Most of us would be familiar with the "dot com" companies, meaning Information Technology (IT) start-ups in most cases. But private equity is not limited to the IT companies; it could be any business, large or small, that is not listed on a public stock exchange, though they are typically of smaller size and not very profitable yet. These private companies typically seek to raise money for the expansion of their businesses.

Investing in private equity is usually done by companies, private equity funds, or HNWIs. Companies could invest for strategic reasons and usually invest with a longer time horizon. Private equity funds and HNWIs are purely profit-driven and tend to have shorter holding periods. Private equity funds can be further subdivided into fund types such as buyout funds, growth funds, venture capital funds, special situation funds, etc., depending on their investment strategy and focus.

PE investing is a long-term investment with horizon of five to ten years minimally. The typical exit strategy of investing in PE is when the private company goes public. But this is not the only route to cash out. A private company could also be merged with or be acquired by other companies, or investors could also receive cash distribution in the form of a dividend from the company through profit generated from its operations or debt raised. If an investor wants to exit a PE investment early, he can go through the secondary market. The secondary market is now starting to develop, though it remains relatively illiquid.

For the purpose of retail and HNWI investing in PE, it is normally restricted to direct investment into individual start-up companies, or through a dedicated PE Fund which will invest into private companies on the individual's behalf. Investing directly into start-up companies could be done at different stages of the start-up's life cycle. There is no clear-cut definition of the stages, but very broadly, one can classify the stages as:

- ◆ Idea/Prototype: This is the earliest stage, where the start-up only has an idea or a prototype to entice investors and friends/families to part with their money.

- ◆ Seed Funding: This is usually the first stage of fund-raising for most start-ups, and the objective is usually to get the start-up to at least break even.

- ◆ Series A, B, C: This is done to grow the revenue, market share and/or profitability of the start-ups.

The earlier that one invests in a start-up, the cheaper the valuation usually. However, it also carries the highest risks as the start-up would not have a stable business or revenue in the early stages. Most investors would not invest at the concept or prototype stage unless there is an extremely compelling idea or the creator/entrepreneur comes with a sterling track record. As such, at the early idea or prototype stage, most would only see friends and families investing.

The seed funding stage is usually when external investors start putting money in. And when the start-up continues to do well, it would then move on to Series A, B and subsequent rounds of fund-raising to grow the business. In every subsequent round of fund-raising, the earlier-round investors' stakes would be diluted, unless they top up their investments. Due to the high failure rate of early stage companies, early stage investors require much higher return multiples in excess of 10 times to be able to justify their investments.

Private equity investing is a highly risky business. Everyone gets to know about the "unicorns" or start-up companies that make it into the $1 billion bracket. For each of these unicorns, there are thousands of start-ups that didn't make it to profitability, dying at varying stages from idea to seed funding to Series X funding. Statistics that look into the failure of start-ups have a survival bias, i.e. only those who survive make it to the statistics. Various studies attempt to quantify the failure rate, and it ranges from 25% to 75%, very roughly speaking, depending on how one quantifies "failure" and when the research was carried out.

Suffice it to say that one should never put all one's eggs in one basket, i.e. invest only in one or a very small number of private companies. The failure rate is so high that one should always diversify into a broad base and a sufficiently large number of companies to ensure that statistics have a chance to play out – that is, you have some successful companies among your portfolio.

Valuing Private Equity

It is difficult to value an unlisted private company, especially one that isn't profitable. Before one invests in a PE company, there are usually comparable companies to reference, unless the idea is really so different from anything else. Some of the common valuation methods include:

- Valuation at each stage of development

- Price to Sales

- Price per Active User

- Discounted Cash Flow (DCF)

The first three methods tend to be used at earlier stages, especially when the start-up isn't profitable. It is not an exact science to say what multiples one should assign for each of the measures, but comparing it with available data out there from similar start-ups might be the best bet. At the idea/prototype or very early rounds, the first method of valuation by stage of development is probably the best guide. How much one values a firm depends on how much value one places on the idea or the ability of the entrepreneur to execute the plan.

As a start-up begins to generate some sales or acquire customers, even without revenue, the next two measures may start to make more sense. Depending on how likely and quickly one could expand the sales and/or customer figures, or monetise the customer base, the price multiples would differ. As the start-up moves to a more advanced stage with positive cash flows, then the DCF method would be applicable, and a firm could be valued more objectively using a classic public equities valuation model.

At the end of the day, how much one values a company is largely dependent on the sector the start-up is in. When the sector is hot, it commands a higher valuation, and vice versa. Another factor that influences valuation is the background of the entrepreneur. A repeat entrepreneur with past successes would command a higher valuation for his start-up even if it were just at the idea phase. After all, the success of a start-up at an early stage is 80% dependent on the entrepreneur and his execution capability. Valuing a start-up is more of an art than a science. Just make sure that you do a little sanity check before you commit to any investments.

Investing in Private Equity

The four ways of gaining exposure to private equity are through:

◈ Direct investments into the private company

◈ Investing in a PE fund

◈ Investing in a Fund of PE funds

◈ Buying shares of listed private equity funds

Direct investment into companies can be for any amount, typically from $10,000 to say $1.5m. For individuals, direct investments are fraught with difficulties. The main problem is access to good companies, and the second is valuing the companies. Most retail individuals have no access to the universe of private companies looking to raise money, simply because the marketplace is too large and dispersed, and there are no dominant exchanges that congregate them for investors.

The popularity of crowdfunding sites like indiegogo.com and kickstarter.com in recent years has certainly made this slightly easier. But how does one do the necessary due diligence for so many private companies out there to know if their valuations are reasonable and worth the investment? Unless one is doing this on a fairly regular basis, it is basically guesswork trying to decide if a company's valuation is rich or cheap. That is not helped by the fact that information on comparable companies is very difficult to come by.

Besides the difficulty in finding promising private companies and in valuing them, it is also difficult to diversify into enough such companies to spread the risk. Remember that private equity investment is highly risky as most of these companies would not see daylight and end up closing, so it is important that one invests into a broad base and a large number of such companies so that even if only 10–20% eventually get listed on an exchange or get bought out, it is enough to pay for the remaining 80–90% which go bust.

If direct investment is too tedious or difficult to do on a part-time basis, the alternative is through investing in PE funds. The difference is obviously that you would pay a management fee and performance fee for the PE funds' professionals to do the work for you. Typical management fees range from 1.5% to 2.5%, while a performance fee (or carried interest) of 20–30% usually applies once the return is above a pre-set minimum hurdle. PE funds also tend to have a long capital "lock-in" period of about 10 years. As professional managers, they have better access to start-ups and private companies looking to raise funds, and they are better able to value them. The best part of it is that they are diversified, so investing into a couple of these PE funds would be equivalent to investing into 10–20 private companies at one go. The main problem with PE funds is the minimum investment size they demand. As PE funds are highly risky due to their investments in private companies, they are usually meant only for accredited investors, typically defined as those with more than $1 million in investable assets other than the home they live in. The minimum investment size is typically $100,000 or more, with many asking for as much as $10 million. Many PE funds have different areas of specialty, so it is important to know which industry or segment you are bullish in before finding the right PE fund. Well-known private equity funds include KKR Fund L.P., run by Kohlberg Kravis Roberts & Co., and various 3i funds run by the 3i Group PLC.

If one considers investing in PE funds still too tedious or undiversified, one can also go the route of sourcing out funds of PE funds! These are funds that farm out investment money into various PE funds based on a pre-specified investment mandate. The advantages are that such a fund will do all the work for you in identifying good PE funds, and for the same capital you invest, you can achieve greater diversification as each fund of PE funds would invest in about a dozen PE funds. The main disadvantage is that the investor pays another layer of costs over investing into the PE funds directly.

Finally, there are some PE funds that are listed on major exchanges such as the NYSE. While one can more easily tap into these listed funds, bear in mind that top-tier PE funds are usually not found on the exchanges.

It is probably clear by now that PE investing is not meant for most people apart from ultra-HNWIs. The returns it promises are higher than public equity returns, but the risks are commensurately high. As such, PE typically occupies only a small weight in a HNWI's asset allocation.

HEDGE FUNDS

A hedge fund pools money from sophisticated investors together and uses leverage to invest in a variety of asset types. The key differences setting it apart from mutual funds, real money funds and private equity funds are that it typically:

- ❖ Uses leverage

- ❖ Uses complex trading algorithms, portfolio construction and risk management tools

- ❖ Invests across asset classes

- ❖ Mostly in liquid assets, but not limited to only developed markets

- ❖ Able to go "long" and "short" assets

- ❖ Not as tightly regulated

Hedge funds got their "hedge" name when they started off helping investors hedge their portfolio against a fall in a particular asset like equity. Over time, the mandate has evolved and the term is used more broadly to represent a unique class of sophisticated funds. Due to their broad investment mandates, and being restricted to sophisticated and accredited investors, hedge funds tend to be less regulated compared to other types of funds. This also allows hedge funds to be far more nimble and adaptable to new markets and instruments.

Hedge funds usually charge "2+20", which means 2% management fee and 20% performance fee. The performance fee usually does not come with a minimum hurdle rate, but might have a "high-water mark", meaning it only charges 20% when its profit exceeds the previous high point. Due to this, there is sometimes incentive for funds who suffer big losses to close down the fund and open a new fund, because they would not be able to have this 20% performance fee until they claw back the losses.

Unlike the long lock-in period for a PE fund, a hedge fund's lock-in is much shorter, typically no more than the first year, with quarterly redemption windows thereafter. During periods of extreme distress, a hedge fund could also raise a "gate" that would stop redemption until conditions normalise, but this is used very sparingly, such as during the Global Financial Crisis of 2008. The main reason for this gate is that during extreme illiquidity that comes with crisis, forced selling due to redemption could be impossible or too damaging to the rest of the fund holders as asset prices are further depressed to illogical levels due to this forced selling.

There are numerous types of strategies employed by hedge funds. The common ones include:

◆ Global Macro

◆ Equity Long/Short

◆ Special Situation/Event-Driven

◆ Distress Debt

◆ Arbitrage/Relative Value

There may be overlap in the strategies, or a fund may operate more than one strategy. Within these strategies, fund managers could be using qualitative and/or quantitative tools to make their investment decisions. They could be focused on a particular asset class like equity, or they could cut across a few asset classes to take advantage of mispricing or pursue a cross-asset strategy to better represent a particular view.

In the past, hedge funds generated market-beating performances after fees rather consistently. However, recent performances have been rather mixed, leading many to question whether hedge funds still deserve to command their hefty fees. Investments in them typically start from at least $250,000, if not $1 million or more. That makes investment in hedge funds almost exclusively for ultra-HNWIs.

Valuing Hedge Funds

Hedge funds are not the most transparent in terms of the assets they invest in. However, they are still obliged to publish performance numbers on a regular basis, which for most funds would be a month-end report. The report will typically talk about their views, their strategies just past and present, their top holdings, and the current and past performance numbers. Besides looking at the profit the funds generate, it is also important to scrutinise the risks they are running. A popular measure is the Sharpe Ratio, which is a measure of excess return over the risk taken. As such, a fund with a higher Sharpe Ratio suggests that the fund is generating more excess return per unit of risk.

Another measure similar to the Sharpe Ratio that is often used is the Sortino Ratio. Unlike the Sharpe Ratio, which does not differentiate the good versus bad volatility of earnings, the Sortino Ratio only considers the volatility of excess returns below a certain rate of return, i.e. it considers the returns relative to the downside risks.

Other common quantitative and qualitative measures to value or compare hedge fund performances include the maximum monthly drawdown, maximum time to recover from a drawdown, risk management process during bouts of poor performances, risk distribution within the fund, key man risks, etc. While past performance does not provide much assurance of future performance, it is nonetheless a good guide to understand the investment process of a hedge fund, and to assess the quality of its managers. Ultimately, it is the manager of the fund that defines the fund.

Most institutional investors require a good three-year performance before investing in a hedge fund. Retail investors and HNWIs can use that as a guide too. It is important to note, however, that three years of good performance does not imply the fund is good, as statistically three years is too short a time to separate the good from the lucky. Therefore it is crucial to also have a good qualitative assessment of the fund manager(s) and the fund before committing any capital.

Investing in Hedge Funds

Hedge fund investment is probably the one with the highest hurdle in terms of investment quantum. Due to the nature of the funds, it is limited to accredited investors only. With investments typically starting from $250,000, it is quite difficult for one with say just a couple of million in investable assets to diversify within this asset class. As such, this is probably meant only for the ultra-HNWIs with net worth of $5m or more. Hedge fund investment is a relatively high-risk investment asset class with no certainty of returns, and it comes with rather high costs annually. It has a place in an ultra-HNWIs' asset allocation, but probably only a small part of 5% or less.

If you have the money, there are big and small hedge funds out there that may or may not be accepting new investment money. The well-known big hedge funds, just to name a few, include Tudor Investment Corporation (run by Paul Tudor Jones), Blue Crest Capital Management, and Fortress Investment Group. Like PE investing, if it is too difficult to decide which hedge fund to invest in, one can also put money in a fund of hedge funds. These funds will source out the best hedge funds out there for you – for a fee.

Conclusion

Besides the traditional asset classes of Stocks, Bonds and Cash, and the popular Real Estate and Foreign Exchange, there are also Commodities, Private Equity and Hedge Fund investments that make up the rest of the asset classes. These latter three are more volatile in nature, and do not have much certainty of capital preservation, even though they promise higher returns generally. Commodities are rather speculative, and are best reserved for only sophisticated investors. As for Private Equity and Hedge Fund investments, they are usually reserved only for accredited investors as they are complex and highly risky, with a high minimum investment quantum and the difficulty of achieving a diversified portfolio.

We have now discussed all the key asset classes available to retail investors in general. We are now ready to discuss some of the more specific investment products available in the market which retail investors can gain access to.

Part II

COMMON
HIGH NET WORTH &
RETAIL PRODUCTS

CHAPTER 5

Equity-Linked Notes

THIS IS ONE OF THE most commonly sold products by Relationship Managers (RMs) of priority banking and private banking. As the name implies, an equity-linked note has two portions – an equity portion and a note portion. It is a "note" in the sense that it pays a coupon or agreed interest rate. The payment of this coupon is contingent on the performance of the equity that is "linked" with this note. If the underlying equity did not achieve the required performance, then the buyer of this product may be left owning the underlying equity instead of receiving the principal and coupon back in cash.

There are numerous variations of Equity-Linked Notes, or ELNs. All of them are typically rated as medium-high to high risk by banks, as they are usually not principal-protected. ELNs are typically structured by combining an interest-earning instrument (e.g. a zero-coupon bond/note or a Certificate of Deposit) and an equity option. The more common ELNs marketed by banks are usually of these three basic types:

◆ Discount ELN with Knock-Out

◆ Callable Daily Range Accrual ELN

◆ ELN with Upside Participation

Most ELNs offered in the market are of the above three types, or slight variations of them. Here is a brief description of what each of them are.

(a) Discount ELN with Knock-Out

A Discount ELN is a structured investment instrument linked to an underlying equity or a basket of equities, targeted towards yield enhancement while enabling the investor to purchase the linked equity at a discount under certain circumstances. At maturity, there is the possibility of the investor being delivered the underlying share or the worst-performing share (in the case of a basket of shares), and he may suffer a substantial or total principal loss if the shares are sold off at a price below the Strike Price.

(b) Callable Daily Range Accrual ELN

A Callable Daily Range Accrual ELN is a structured investment instrument linked to underlying shares subject to risk of principal loss. The Issuer may early-redeem the ELN prior to maturity under certain Knock-Out conditions. The first coupon is fixed and subsequent coupon amounts are dependent on the performance of the underlying shares. Typically, for each day the stocks trade within a pre-specified range, a higher interest rate would be earned. At maturity there is a possibility of delivery into the underlying share or the worst-performing share (for basket of shares) where the investor may suffer a substantial or total principal loss if the shares are sold off at a price below the Strike Price.

(c) ELN with Upside Participation

An ELN with upside participation is often a note linked to the upside performance of a stock or a basket of stocks. Its coupon is a function of the percentage return of the underlying stocks. For example, an ELN with 70% upside participation would get a return equivalent to 70% of the upside performance of the underlying stocks, with a return usually floored at 0 if the underlying stock were to decline. As such, this structure is usually principal-protected at maturity. However, depending on the investor's conviction and aggressiveness, this ELN could also be structured as a non-principal-protected ELN, where the investor gets back typically a fixed percentage of its principal (e.g. 95%) if the underlying stocks decline in exchange for a higher participation rate.

The above descriptions are usually too abstract for the average person to comprehend fully. It is always easier to understand what a product is by starting from a simple example.

Example of an ELN

Here's a sample offering of a Discount ELN with Knock-Out from a bank with a presence in Singapore:

Discount ELN with Knock-Out	
Equity-Linked Basket:	OCBC, DBS, UOB
Tenor:	6 months
Coupon/Interest Rate:	5%
Strike Price:	95% of initial price
Barrier Price:	100% of initial price

Final Share Price: The closing price of each and every share in the basket on the final valuation date (typically three days before the maturity date, but depends on the exchange the shares are traded on).

Early Redemption: This occurs when ALL the shares in the basket trade at or above the Barrier Price on a particular day during the Observation Period (which typically starts one month after the purchase of the ELN, and ends on the final valuation date). If this happens, the buyer of the ELN will be paid the interest rate up to that day and the ELN terminates.

Redemption Amount on Maturity Date: If no Early Redemption has occurred, then on maturity date the buyer of the ELN would either be getting their invested cash with interest back, or getting delivered the worst-performing (percentage-wise) shares instead of their invested cash, depending on where the Final Share Price of each of the stocks in the basket is:

- If each and every Final Share Price ≥ Strike Price, the investor will receive cash plus interest.

- If ANY of the Final Share Prices < Strike Price, the investor will receive the shares of the worst-performing share in the basket.

Let's put some numbers into this example and examine the potential of this ELN. Some computations may be deliberately simplified so that we can stay focused on the main considerations of the pros and cons of an ELN.

Share	Initial Share Price	Strike Price	Barrier Price
DBS Group Holdings Ltd	17.88	16.986	17.88
Oversea-Chinese Banking Corp	9.42	8.949	9.42
United Overseas Bank Ltd	20.06	19.057	20.06

For ease of illustration, let's assume for now that all three shares trade similarly in terms of percentage up-move and down-move, i.e. all three shares can be similarly represented by one line for each of the scenarios in the chart below:

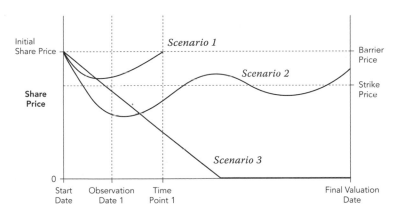

Let's analyse what is happening in each scenario:

Scenario 1: Early redemption

At Time Point 1, all the shares close at or above the Barrier Price. An Early Redemption Event occurs and the contract is terminated early.

The holder of the ELN will receive the Specified Denomination in cash on the Early Redemption Date.

A fixed Interest amount is also payable on each Interest Payment Date on and prior to the Early Redemption Event.

Scenario 2: Investor gets back cash

Between Observation Date 1 and Final Valuation Date, the Shares close below the Barrier Price. No Early Redemption Event occurs.

At maturity, as the Final Share Prices of the Shares are at or above the Strike Prices, the holder of the ELN will receive the Specified Denomination in cash.

A fixed Interest amount is also payable on each Interest Payment Date up to and including the Maturity Date.

Scenario 3: Investor gets delivered shares

Between Observation Date 1 and Final Valuation Date, the Shares close below the Barrier Price. No Early Redemption Event occurs.

As the Final Share Prices of the Shares are close to zero, the holder of a Security will have a mark-to-market loss equal to the Specified Denomination per Security, as they will receive Shares (number of Shares = Specified Denomination per Security / Strike Price).

A fixed Interest amount is also payable on each Interest Payment Date up to and including the Maturity Date.

In Scenario 3 the holder of the ELN will lose an amount equal to the amount invested into the ELN.

Now assuming an investor starts with investing $100,000 in this ELN, here are the potential gains or losses in the various scenarios:

When is Barrier (Time Point 1) triggered?	Scenario 1 *Early redemption event*	Scenario 2 *Investor gets back cash*	Scenario 3 *Investor gets delivered shares*
In 1 month (start of Observation Period)	$417 ($100,000 × 5% × 1/12)	N/A	N/A
In 3 months	$1,250 ($100,000 × 5% × 3/12)	N/A	N/A
In 5.5 months	$2,292 ($100,000 × 5% × 5.5/12)	N/A	N/A
No Barrier event in all 6 months	N/A	$2,500 ($100,000 × 5% × 6/12)	−$97,500 (max loss, if share is worth 0; being $2500 in interest earned less the $100,000 capital loss)

Scenario 3 is obviously an extreme scenario that most of us normally do not expect to see, especially in this case where the underlying shares are three large domestic systemically important banks in Singapore. However, what if the underlying shares are not these three banks in another ELN structure, but are linked to some highly volatile small-cap stocks?

The thought of losing one's capital entirely is scary, but is a distinct possibility that should not be ignored.

Granted, barring a major crisis or fraud with the underlying company of the share, most times if Scenario 3 were to happen, the share price on the delivered share is seldom that far away from the 100% it started with. Let's modify Scenario 3 slightly and assume that instead of the share being worth 0, the worst-performing share in the basket on Maturity Date is trading at 90% of the initial price. In this case, the loss to the investor is more manageable, at –$7,500, being interest earned ($2,500) minus capital loss (10% × $100,000).

Let's also assume that should the barrier event happen in Scenario 1, it would be roughly in the middle of the life of the ELN, that is, at the end of the third month, for simplicity. We now have three scenarios with the following payout profile:

Scenario 1 Early redemption event in 3 months	Scenario 2 Investor gets back cash	Scenario 3 Investor gets delivered shares that are trading at 90%
$1,250 ($100,000 × 5% × 3/12)	$2,500 ($100,000 × 5% × 6/12)	–$7,500 (being $2,500 in interest earned less the $10,000 capital loss)

Now we have three possible scenarios with a clear payout in each of the scenarios. If we further make a simple and totally unscientific assumption that the three scenarios all have an equal chance of happening, what is then the expected payout in this structure?

$$
\begin{aligned}
\text{Expected payout} \ = \ & (1/3 \times \$1250) + \\
& (1/3 \times \$2500) + \\
& (1/3 \times -\$7500) \\
= \ & -\$1,250
\end{aligned}
$$

This means one should expect to lose $1,250 investing in this product, based on the above assumptions.

That sounds ridiculous, as not many would invest in a product with negative expected payout, so maybe our assumptions of probability were overly simplistic. We could use simulation models like Monte Carlo to get a more scientific probability of each of the three scenarios happening. The mathematics is rather complex and goes beyond my intention to be as simple as possible to understand and to evaluate the investment at hand. As such, let's tweak the parameters and examine the expected payout in another possible scenario.

What if Scenario 3 happens when the shares were trading on valuation date just below the Strike Price, which is the best that could happen to an investor under Scenario 3?

Expected Payout if Scenario 3 has shares delivered when the worst-performing share is at 94.9% of the initial price, keeping the other two scenarios unchanged:

$$
\begin{aligned}
\text{Expected payout} \\
= \ & (1/3 \times \$1250) + (1/3 \times \$2500) + \\
& (1/3 \times [\$2500 - \{100\% - 94.9\%\} \times \$100{,}000]) \\
= \ & (1/3 \times \$1250) + (1/3 \times \$2500) + (1/3 \times -\$2600) \\
= \ & \$383
\end{aligned}
$$

So if we kept the probability of each scenario happening as equal for simplicity, and assuming the most likely outcome in Scenario 3 to be one of "least loss", i.e. the shares trading just below the Strike Price (94.9% compared to Strike Price of 95%) on final valuation date, one should expect to earn $383 investing in this product.

This translates to an expected annualised yield of 0.76% (being $383/$100,000 × 12/6).

"Not so bad", you might say to yourself, given the extremely low deposit rates in the current interest rate environment. You could tweak an infinite amount of the parameters above, like the probability of each scenario playing out. Even better, put in parameters of what you think is likely to happen and see what the expected payout might be.

You may feel that this exercise generates just an expected return based on some overly simplistic assumptions that we made. But isn't it better to know how much you are likely to get paid based on your view and assumptions then just buy without even knowing the expected payout, regardless of how simplistic the assumptions might be?

Don't be surprised if you find yourself facing only a small positive or even negative expected return based on your assumptions once you go through this simple exercise! If that happens, at least you can decide whether to proceed with the ELN instead of feeling stupid later on when you realise that you didn't make much money even when your views turned out right!

We have just gone through an example of a common type of ELN. The other ELN types could also be similarly broken down into simple understandable bits to estimate the expected payout.

We mentioned at the start of the chapter that ELNs typically involve an interest-bearing instrument and an equity option. In this ELN example, the bank structuring the ELN would most likely be buying a zero-coupon bond and selling an equity put option on behalf of the customer. That is, the investor (you) have sold the equity put option, meaning you have given the right to sell you the stock at a pre-specified price to the buyer of the option.

Not all ELNs involve selling an equity put. For example, the ELN with upside participation involves buying an equity call option. For simplicity, our analysis in this chapter focuses mostly on the example of a Discount ELN with Knock-Out, i.e. selling volatility.

What Should I Consider Before Buying the ELN?

To help answer that question, let's examine the investment objectives as stated in the term sheet of this bank's ELN. The ELN is designed for investors who:

- Have a six-month positive view on *all* shares in the basket;

- Expect all shares in the basket to trade within a pre-determined range of parameters, i.e. expect the Closing Share Prices to fluctuate between the respective Strike Prices and the Barrier Prices during the life of the Security; and

- Are prepared to directly hold the worst-performing share in the basket should the Final Share Price be less than the Strike Price.

The investment objectives suggest the need for a *view* of the shares by the investor. Note that it doesn't say anything about the (higher) interest rate that it pays. It emphasises that the investor should have a positive view of all shares in the basket, but clearly not too positive because the investor should also expect that these shares trade within a range for the entire tenure. In this example, the range is 95% to 100% of the initial price, which is expressing a view that the shares should not *all* appreciate from the initial level. If the investor is wrong, he should be prepared to hold the worst-performing share in the basket.

(a) To buy the ELN, we should have a view on the *trading range* of the underlying shares

So judging from the investment objectives, it seems that the motivation for buying an ELN is not so much about the higher interest rates, but everything about the underlying shares. An investor should have a view on the shares in the basket first and foremost, be willing to bet on its share price movement in the entire period, and not mind holding it should the shares fall in price. The higher interest rate is an afterthought, it appears, and should merely act as a "sweetener" or perhaps a "hedge" in case the investor is wrong, either in his view that the shares should trade in a range or that the shares will not fall off the cliff.

Is owning the shares typically the main motivation of an ELN investor? In my conversations with bank RMs, investors seem to be first attracted by the high advertised interest rates of the ELN. So an ELN with low interest rates would not be popular, irrespective of the underlying shares.

Informed investors would generally assess the shares in the basket to consider (1) if they mind owning the shares; (2) if they feel that the shares are going up or down in the next few months; (3) if the interest rate offered is high enough to justify the risk they are taking.

Considerations (1) and (2) are subjective, and very much dependent on investors' individual past experience with the shares or shaped by their views of the broader market/industry/shares direction. Consideration (3) is typically subject to an investor's "feeling" of how volatile the shares are, which directly affects how likely he is to be left holding the shares come maturity date. Generally the higher the perceived volatility, the higher the investor would expect to be compensated via a higher interest rate.

This concept of "volatility" can be objectively measured. The value of "historical volatility" of the underlying shares can be obtained from data providers like Reuters and Bloomberg. Without going into too much technical detail here, the "volatility" of each share can be expressed in percentage terms, which are typically way above 10% annualised. The "correlation" of the movement of each of the underlying shares could also be calculated. The volatility and correlation combined will tell us how the basket of shares is likely to be trading in the future, assuming of course it behaves in the same way going forward as it did in the past.

Suffice it to say at this juncture that the more volatile the shares, the higher the yield that the ELN would pay. This is intuitively right too, as the higher the volatility, the greater the likelihood of Scenarios 1 and 3 playing out, which are less profitable scenarios for the investor compared to Scenario 2. Put another way, by buying into this ELN, the investor is effectively "selling volatility" in exchange for a higher yield. As such, the higher the "absolute value" of volatility, the more the investor should be compensated by selling at a higher value. If one goes into how an ELN is structured, one would also see that the underlying structure of an ELN involves among other things, selling "put options" on the shares. It is through this act of selling that the "structure" of ELN is able to enhance the yield of the ELN, i.e. pay more than the market interest rate.

Now that we understand that buying an ELN involves selling the volatility of the underlying shares, we can add the following:

*(b) To buy the ELN, we should have a view on the **volatility** of the underlying shares going forward*

Many friends and potential investors of ELNs tell me that it is too difficult to forecast the direction and volatility of the shares in the next month, let alone forecast for as long as three or six months, the typical tenure of an ELN. Most investors just consider whether they are positive or bullish on the shares. If they are, they tell me that they would be "happy" to be able to buy the shares at 95% in the worst-case scenario of the ELN, which is a huge savings of 5% from the current level. Does this sound familiar?

Of course! Everyone loves a discount, and is happy to buy things cheaper than current market price. But now put yourself in this situation: It is two months later, and the share(s) that you would be "happy" to be able to buy at 95% are trading at 93% of the initial price. Do you still feel as happy?

"It's okay, the shares will trade back up later, after all I don't own the shares currently and there is still a good four months before the ELN matures", one might reason. You are smiling now because chances are you have heard that before too!

In all likelihood, the investor is less happy as there is a higher chance now that he owns the shares at a price (95%) that is higher than the current price (93%). The fact that he does not "own" the shares at that juncture does not change the fact that the shares are no longer trading at a discount to the initial price of 100%, and thus the investor is no longer buying at a discount but now at a premium! The nice feeling from two months ago is long gone, and the investor is really faced with a situation of "What to do if I own the shares at 95% in four months' time?"

As a prudent investor, one should be thinking of hedging the risk of potential losses. However, as I have seen in most retail investors, hedging the risk of share price falls is rather rare. Most would just sit tight and hope for the share to rebound. Without going into more technicalities, as I have already highlighted that buying an ELN is effectively selling volatility, one would find that to hedge a "short volatility" position requires one to buy high and sell low, which is extremely difficult for a retail investor to do even if they know how to!

All this is too difficult for retail investors to comprehend or act on. At the end of the day, they generally ignore these difficulties, and invest in the ELN if the interest rate they get is high enough to "hedge" the risk of the falling shares. They hope that even if the shares were to fall, they would not fall by too much, and that they would be happy to own the shares for the long term.

(c) To buy the ELN, we should have a view on the
interest rate *offered to compensate for*
the risk of falling shares

In summary, we have now established the premise of when one should buy the ELN. You are likely to be an investor who is positive on the underlying shares in the long run, thinks the shares would likely trade in a narrow range in the (short) term of the ELN, thinks that the shares would likely be less volatile than the immediate past, *and* thinks that the interest rate being paid is high enough to compensate for the risk taken.

Other Considerations Before Buying the ELN

We have covered the key considerations one should have before buying the ELN. Again, before you rush to call your Relationship Manager to buy the ELN, here I highlight some other points an investor typically does not think about:

- ◆ Other than the three scenarios, are there other scenarios to consider?

- ◆ What is the right size to invest in an ELN?

- ◆ Single-stock or multi-stock ELN?

- ◆ What to think about if you are delivered the shares under Scenario 3?

Let's examine each of the above in a little more detail.

(a) Other than the three scenarios, are there other scenarios to consider?

Most investors hope for Scenario 2 (get back cash at maturity) to play out. This makes sense, as it is the scenario with the best payout. If the investor remains positive on the underlying shares at the maturity of the ELN, he could still take the cash and interest paid and proceed to buy the desired shares at below 100%. Job well done!

Many investors are realistic enough to know that they cannot simply expect Scenario 2 to play out without paying heed to Scenarios 1 and 3. Obviously, due to the positive payout, Scenario 1 is preferred to Scenario 3. And if the investor is prepared to hold the shares come hell or high water, then we have all our angles and possibilities considered and covered. Right?

In a typical ELN, where two or more stocks are grouped in a basket, these stocks do not always perform the same during the ELN tenure. Investors also tend to prefer some stocks to others, and may not like all the shares in the basket equally. Very often, even in Scenario 2, some shares of the basket tend to do better than the others, and could be trading above 100% while the rest trade between 95% and 100%. In Scenario 3, investor is delivered the worst-performing share of the basket only, not *all* the shares in equal proportion. It is important to also remember that only one stock in the basket needs to trade below 95% for the share to be delivered, irrespective of how the rest of the shares do. In Scenario 1, while all shares in the basket would trade above 100% for the ELN to be early redeemed, some or all of the shares in the basket could be trading at a lot higher than 100% at that time.

In each of the three scenarios, there may be occasions where the investor's most favoured share in the basket is trading a lot *higher* than 100%, say 110%. All that the investor gets would be the promised interest rate for the period the ELN is held in the best case, or delivered the worst-performing share in the worst case. How would you feel if you were that investor? Not so good, I bet, as you would have missed the opportunity to buy the shares at 100%, and now it would cost you much more to buy the same shares. The interest you earned, even in the best Scenario 2, would merely soften the blow, not eliminate the pain of missing the opportunity to buy.

This is the opportunity cost of *not* buying the shares right from the beginning, at 100%. This is an opportunity cost because the investment objectives state that you should buy the ELN only if you don't mind owning the shares, so we must assume that owning the shares at a discount might be the main motivation of investing in the ELN.

In dollar terms, it is the difference in price at which the desired shares are trading at then, minus the interest rate return one has from the ELN. In the example above, if the investor originally intended to buy OCBC, and OCBC is trading at 110% or $10.36 come ELN maturity, the opportunity cost would be:

[($10.36 – $9.42) × number of shares investor originally intended to buy] – $2,500

Put another way, investors who got their wish of Scenario 2 granted might still be unhappy if they missed their opportunity to buy their most favoured shares in the basket at the starting price.

To help you think through when you should be buying an ELN, have a look at the two tables on the following pages before you make that call to the RM.

◆ Table A is for an ELN that involves selling volatility.

◆ Table B is for an ELN with upside participation, which involves buying volatility.

Note that S/T (Short Term) is defined as the period between inception and the first observation date; while L/T (Long Term) is defined as the period between the first and last observation dates.

(b) What is the right size to invest in an ELN?

This question appears trivial but many investors actually get it wrong. Why? Two main reasons:

◆ There is a minimum investment sum required by the priority or private bank.

◆ Investors think in terms of how much cash they hope to earn the higher interest on.

In the first instance, most banks have a minimum investment requirement of at least $100,000 per ELN. As such, investors have no choice but to gather at least the minimum sum if they want to invest in it.

TABLE A
For a typical Single-stock ELN with Delivery Strike at 95% and Knock-Out at 103% – Should you buy it?

Your view of the stock?	L/T Bearish ↘	L/T Sideways →	L/T Bullish ↗
S/T Bearish ↘	**Best:** Paid high yield till maturity, stocks not delivered **Worst:** Stocks delivered **Do it if...** yield is very high or you really want the stock because you will be delivered the stock if your bearish views are right! Consider picking another stock or wait for lower stock level before doing this ELN	**Best:** Paid high yield till maturity **Worst:** Stocks delivered **Do it if...** you think stock will trade slightly lower so you could earn the high yield till maturity; you are not that bearish on the stock, but you won't mind owning the stock even if delivered	**Best:** Paid high yield till maturity **Worst:** K/O early before maturity **Do it if...** you are mildly positive on the stock long-term but think it will correct first; happy to just receive high yield for a while and not own the stock even though you are bullish
S/T Sideways →	**Best:** Paid high yield till maturity **Worst:** Stocks delivered **Do it if...** you are long-term bearish but want the high yield till maturity; you don't mind owning the stock if delivered despite your bearishness	**Best:** Paid high yield till maturity **Worst:** If you are right, you won't be K/O or delivered the stock **Do it if...** you think the stock is just going to be really stable and boring; this is perfect for ELN!	**Best:** Paid high yield for two or more observation periods **Worst:** K/O at the second observation date **Do it if...** yield is really high or you are only very mildly positive on the stock long-term as K/O is likely before maturity; happy not to own the stock even though you are bullish
S/T Bullish ↗	**Best:** Paid high yield till maturity **Worst:** K/O at the first observation date or stocks delivered **Do it if...** you are only very mildly bullish on the stock short-term and do not expect to be K/O early and so paid high yield till maturity; you don't mind owning the stock if delivered	**Best:** Paid high yield for two or more observation periods or till maturity **Worst:** K/O at the first observation date **Do it if...** yield is really high or you are only very mildly bullish on the stock short-term and do not expect to be K/O early; you hope to be paid the high yield for as long as possible	**Best:** Paid high yield for two or more observation periods **Worst:** K/O at the first observation date **Do it if...** *only if* yield is crazy high because if your bullish views are right, you will be K/O very quickly! Consider buying the stock instead!

TABLE B
For a typical Single-stock ELN with Upside Participation – Should you buy it?

Your view of the stock?	L/T Bearish ↘	L/T Sideways →	L/T Bullish ↗
S/T Bearish ↘	**NO!** You are clearly bearish on this stock, why are you thinking of an ELN with *upside* participation?	**No** You are not bullish on the stock at all, so this ELN with upside participation is not suitable.	**Perhaps** If overall you are mildly positive about the stock, this ELN is fine as you suffer no loss when it first declines. However, if you are confident the stock would first decline, consider doing it later when you think stock is near bottom.
S/T Sideways →	**No** You are not bullish on the stock at all, so this ELN with upside participation is not suitable.	**No** You are not bullish on the stock at all, so this ELN with upside participation is not suitable.	**Yes** If you are right on the long-term positive view of the stock, this ELN would reward you.
S/T Bullish ↗	**Perhaps** If overall you are mildly positive about the stock despite the long-term bearishness, this ELN is fine. However, if you are confident the stock will decline in the longer term, consider doing this ELN for a shorter tenure to match your view?	**Yes** If you are right on the bullish view of the stock, this ELN would reward you.	**YES!** You will certainly make money if your bullish view is right. Due to your bullishness, you could also consider buying the underlying stock directly to maximise your potential gain.

In the second instance, the ELN is a product where one should first be thinking of the underlying shares one wants to own (remember the investment objectives?), *not* how much cash one hopes to earn the higher interest on. ELN is *not* a Time Deposit.

In both instances, you should ask yourself this basic question: Is $100,000 invested in *one* company's stock too much for your portfolio? The answer depends on how much wealth you have, how you diversify your overall portfolio and stock portfolio, how much risk you are comfortable with in any single stock, etc. Suffice it to say that unless you are a millionaire, or you are a very active investor/speculator, you are unlikely to be comfortable with having $100,000 or more invested in any single stock. So if you are caught in the situation of Scenario 3, are you prepared to own the $100,000 or more worth of the single worst-performing shares when they are delivered to you? If yes, you are fine. If not, you might want to consider right-sizing your investment amount in the ELN.

(c) Single-stock or Multi-stock ELN?

In our earlier ELN example, we made the convenient assumption that the three stocks would trade exactly like each other. That almost never happens in real life. Having an ELN with a basket of three stocks makes it far more complicated to analyse. The complication arises from the correlation between the three stocks. In a single-stock ELN, one does not have to think of correlation. Here's a table to examine the pros and cons of a multi-stock Discount ELN with Knock-Out:

Pros and Cons of Multi-stock ELN	Implication
Pros: Less likely to be Knocked-Out because *all* the underlying stocks have to trade above the Barrier Price for you to be K/O.	Implies that it is good if the stocks in the basket are uncorrelated or lowly correlated to one another.
Cons: More likely to be delivered because just *one* of the underlying stocks needs to trade below the Strike Price for you to be delivered that stock.	Implies that it is good if the stocks in the basket are highly correlated to one another, so if one of the stocks goes up, all the stocks in the basket are likely to trade up together.

The above table clearly describes why there is no clear-cut answer to whether one should buy a multi-stock ELN with highly correlated or uncorrelated underlying stocks.

So when should an investor buy a single-stock ELN and when should he consider buying a multi-stock ELN? To answer that question, let's revisit the objective of the specific Discount ELN with Knock-Out:

> You are likely to be an investor who is positive on the underlying shares in the long run, thinks the shares would likely trade in a narrow range in the (short) term of the ELN, thinks that the shares would likely be less volatile than the immediate past, and thinks that the interest rate you are being paid is high enough to compensate for the risk you take.

The clearest answer lays in the first line: one should be positive on the underlying shares – not just one but *all* of them

– if one is to do a multi-stock ELN. In our example above for the three Singapore banks ELN, you must want to own any of the three stocks just as much, or at the minimum not hate owning any of them. If you don't want to own any of them, they should not be in your ELN.

Secondly, you should have a view of each of the stocks' trading range and volatility going forward. What remains thereafter is the interest rate you are being paid, and that's the easiest part as you only need to compare the interest you will be paid if you do a single-bank ELN versus a multi-bank ELN like the above. You could go through the same simple computation for the expected payout and compare which makes more sense.

Personally, given the lack of processing power a retail or high net worth investor has, I am of the view that it is simpler to buy single-stock ELN. It is always good to know with reasonable certainty which stock I could be owning if delivered at maturity rather than be kept guessing or, worse still, miss buying all the underlying stocks because I thought I would own one of them! I would personally only consider multi-stock ELNs if the promised interest rates are much higher.

(d) What to think about if you are delivered the shares under Scenario 3?

What if you really don't want to have $100,000 or more worth of one share delivered under Scenario 3 but would still like to invest in the ELN that has a minimum investment amount of $100,000? That does not mean you cannot invest in the ELN, but it does mean that you must have a plan to reduce your holding of that share in that event. You should consider this plan upfront, and not consider it only when given the shares on maturity.

What most investors do not think about or realise is that the shares, if delivered, are typically delivered to the bank's account. They are held in the bank's "nominee account" on behalf of the investor. The investors can't sell the shares through their regularly used specialised stockbrokers; they usually have to sell through the bank's securities broking house, which may have high brokerage charges.

Alternatively, they could check with their RMs to see if they could transfer the delivered shares into a custodian like CDP in Singapore so that they could then go through their usual brokerages to sell. If the investor intends to hold on to all or some of the shares for a longer period, it is also worth checking the bank's charges for custodianship of the shares. These charges, while not significant in most cases, do add on to the cost of the ELN structure in the worst-case Scenario 3. You may be already unhappy being delivered the worst-performing shares, the last thing you want is to find out at that juncture that you are charged for holding the shares or selling them!

Conclusion

I have set out the many considerations for an investor before investing in an ELN. While I have only gone through one of the three most common ELN structures, the considerations for investing in all the ELN types are similar. One does not need to go into complicated simulations and mathematical formulas to determine the expected payout, but can simply assign one's own probability of occurrence for each scenario and arrive at the expected payout.

The expected payout is but one of the more objective considerations. Due to the many complicated conditions in ELNs, it is easy to lose sight of why one is investing in ELNs. To avoid disappointment, there are many other points an investor should consider before taking the plunge. Investors should know of these considerations before investing if they don't want to end up in an unhappy situation, including the (ideal?) scenario where they get the payout in cash on maturity, but find that they have missed the bull run in the underlying stocks that they wanted to own!

CHAPTER 6

Dual Currency Investments

THERE ARE MANY FORMS of investment in currencies, or foreign exchange (FX) as they are more commonly called, available in the market. One can trade FX most directly by buying one currency and selling another currency through a bank or online trading platform. In this chapter, the focus is on one of the most commonly sold products in the priority and private banking world – Dual Currency Investments, or DCI for short.

Some banks have a different name for this product, for example Currency Linked Investments (CLI). They are essentially the same product, with little to no difference. I will be using the acronym DCI for the rest of the chapter.

Any FX or currency investment always involves two currencies. It's no different in a DCI. The key difference between a DCI and a traditional FX spot transaction is that one does not immediately convert from one currency into another currency on the start date. It is probably more similar to an FX Forward transaction, except that the conversion into another currency on maturity date is contingent on a pre-set condition, typically on the relative performance of the two currencies. In short, DCI is a short-term investment where the principal and interests will be paid in a "base" currency or the "alternate" currency, at a pre-agreed FX rate.

The most common DCI is one where an investor is invested in one currency (e.g. USD), commits to holding it for a fixed tenure (typically one week to six months), earns a pre-agreed interest rate (typically higher than the risk-free rate), and on maturity is paid back this currency plus interest *or* is given this same amount in another currency (e.g. GBP) if the exchange rate of the second currency falls below a certain pre-determined level. The usual minimum investment amount is $50,000.

A DCI is usually individually custom-designed by the bank based on the investor's needs. The investor decides on the two currencies in question, the tenure, the "strike price" where one currency will be converted to another, and then the bank will determine the corresponding interest rate that would apply based on those parameters.

Example of a DCI

Investment Amount:	US$100,000
Base Currency:	USD
Alternate Currency:	GBP
Interest Rate:	8%
Tenure:	1 month
Current GBP/USD:	1.55 (this is market convention; it means £1 = US$1.55)
Trigger Level GBP/USD:	1.53 (this means GBP falling in value, as £1 = US$1.53)

On valuation date, which is typically two business days before maturity date, two scenarios are possible:

Scenario 1:
*GBP/USD is **above** the trigger level of 1.53*

The investor will receive on maturity date in the base currency of USD the principal plus interest:

$100,000 + ($100,000 × 8% × 1/12) = US$100,666.67

Scenario 2 :
*GBP/USD is **at or below** the trigger level of 1.53*

The investor will receive on maturity date in the alternate currency of GBP the principal + interest of US$100,666.67 converted at the trigger rate of 1.53:

US$100,666.67 / 1.53 = £65,795.21

In this scenario, if the investor chooses to convert the alternate currency back to the base currency immediately, he may incur a loss in principal depending on where the spot FX level is at that time. For example, if the spot market for GBP/USD FX is trading at 1.50 at that time, and investor chooses to convert the whole amount from GBP back to USD, he will receive

£65,795.21 × 1.50 = US$98,692.82

This would represent a loss to the investor, as it is lower than the initial principal amount of US$100,000.

What Should I Consider Before Investing in a DCI Product?

DCI is a relatively straightforward product. An investor needs to consider relatively fewer things as compared to many other products. In my view, the DCI investor should:

- Have a view on the relative movement between the two currencies

- Have a view on whether the interest rate offered fairly compensates for the risks

- Must be prepared to hold the alternate currency should it fall in value

To have a view on the relative movement and the fairness of the interest rate on offer, an investor should ideally have a sense of where the interest rates for each of the base and alternate currencies are. Knowing these interest rates levels would obviously provide a rough indication of whether the interest rate being offered makes sense. More importantly, the difference in the interest rate levels of the two currencies could also tell which currency is theoretically likely to trade stronger or weaker to compensate for the interest rate differential. As a guide, based on the theory of interest rate parity, the currency with the higher interest rate is expected to fall with respect to the currency with the lower interest rate.

It follows that an investor must be incentivised to hold the currency with lower interest rate, and so he must be compensated by a higher value (higher FX) over time for it. This

concept is reflected in the Forward FX Rate of the two currencies. In this example, as GBP pays a slightly higher interest
rate to the near 0 rate of the USD, the one-month forward
rate of GBP should be lower than 1.55 (e.g. 1.5490) to compensate for it.

The market forward FX rate should really be what the
investor focuses on. Put another way, this is the market's the-
oretical value of where the FX of the two currencies might
be trading at that future point of time. As such, an investor
should pick the trigger level using this as a reference, and not
just look at the current FX spot level.

How is it that an investor is able to get a much higher
interest rate in this structure? A Singapore bank's product
summary for DCI (or CLI, by its naming convention) states
the following:

> CLI is designed for customers seeking higher yield
> enhancement. Part of or all of the payout payable by
> the Bank on the CLI represents the premium payable
> by the Bank in consideration of the currency option
> granted by the customer to the Bank.

What did the customer grant to the bank? To understand
that, one must first realise that the investor is really selling
"volatility" of the underlying FX, which is GBP/USD in this
example. Here the investor is effectively selling a currency
option, more precisely a GBP Put/USD Call strike at 1.53.
The premium received from this selling is used to enhance
the yield of the DCI. Put another way, an investor who buys
a DCI is also expressing a view that the volatility of the FX
between the two currencies is going to fall.

What is the main motivation of a DCI investor? It is usually the higher yields. Besides that, some investors choose to express their FX views via DCI instead of through a traditional FX trading account, especially in the case of retail investors who are not too sophisticated or not bothered with having a separate FX trading account.

How does the investor then choose the two currencies? Many investors pick currencies that have the highest volatility, or that they have strong views on. Others pick currencies where they have a real need. For example, if the investor has a mortgage to service in Sydney, he might pick the Australian Dollar (AUD) as one of the two currencies. If he has a child who is studying in the UK, he may be more inclined to pick GBP. This is understandable, as they would not mind owning the alternate currency on maturity if they have some use for it anyway. Their thinking is that if the alternate currency falls in value, they would own the alternate currency at a lower pre-determined level (1.53 in our example) while still being paid a high interest rate, so it is a win-win for them. If the alternate currency does not fall, well then they have earned a good return with the high interest rate too. There is little downside for them, so they reason.

It sounds fair and reasonable. Except that in real life, we see many investors who claimed that they have real need for the alternate currency do the reverse in the DCI whenever they are delivered the alternate currency. So in our example above, if GBP/USD falls below 1.53, say to 1.50, the investor will be delivered GBP. With the GBP in hand, the investor will then buy another DCI with GBP now as the base currency, and USD as the alternate currency, at a strike of say 1.52 (i.e. GBP to be stronger and USD weaker). If the GBP recovers against the USD above 1.52 come maturity day in another month, say back to 1.55, they would be delivered into USD, and being paid the higher interest rate in the process. They are back!

Let's look at the mathematics. In this second DCI example, let's keep it simple by assuming the same 8% interest rate for one month. At maturity, GBP/USD goes back up to 1.55, against a trigger level of 1.52, so the investor is delivered into USD now. The investor will receive on maturity date in the alternate currency of USD the principal plus interest in GBP converted at the rate of 1.52:

$$[£65,795.21 + (65,795.21 \times 8\% \times 1/12)] \times 1.52$$
$$= US\$100,675.44$$

What has the investor made in these two months of volatility where GBP/USD went from 1.55 to 1.50 and then back to 1.55? The investor earned US$675.44 in our example, which translates to a yield of about 4.05% on an annualised basis. Not bad, you would say. Indeed. If one is lucky enough to have the two currencies trading up and down in a narrow range for two months, one should in theory be rewarded well. That is because the investor is right! He is selling volatility and if the currencies are trading in a narrow range, he should be rewarded. If he repeats this and each time the same outcome happens and GBP/USD keeps trading between 1.50 and 1.55, the investor would on average earn over 4% for that period.

"All good, I can do this all year", the investor thinks. Life is never so simple. What if the GBP fall against the USD does not stop at 1.50 but goes on to say 1.45 next? If one looks at the GBP chart below, one would know that this is distinctly possible, and one does not need a crisis for a move of that magnitude to happen.

GBP/USD weekly chart

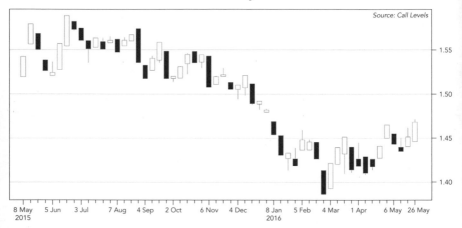

In the scenario of GBP continuing to fall, if the investor had done the reverse leg of the DCI (base currency GBP, alternate currency USD), he would still have his money in GBP, as GBP weakened against USD. He would have earned the high interest for that month, but his GBP would be worth a lot less in USD terms compared to his starting point. If the investor does not have an underlying need for the GBP, he is now faced with a big loss.

Currencies can go one direction in a big way for a long time. The 15-year chart of AUD/USD below, which is another

AUD/USD 15-year chart

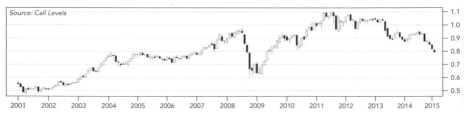

popular choice of currencies for DCI, is a good illustration of this.

Let's summarise the premise of when one should buy the DCI:

> You are likely to be an investor who thinks that the exchange rate between the base and alternate currencies will trade in a narrow range or be less volatile than the immediate past, does not mind owning the alternate currency *and* thinks that the interest rate you are being paid is high enough to compensate for the risk you take.

Other Considerations Before Investing in DCI

We have identified what an investor in DCI is likely to have considered. There are a couple more points to think about.

(a) Is the investor's "home" currency the same as the base currency?

All this while, we have conveniently assumed that the investor already has the base currency, which may or may not be the investor's home currency. What if the investor's "home", which is where he lives, earns his living, and calls home, is *not* the same as the "base"? In that case, there is a third angle, which is the FX movement between the home currency and the base and/or alternate currency!

If the investor is comfortable to have a part of his wealth diversified into another (base) currency for an extended period of time and not worry about the FX movement, then that is fine. Otherwise, the timing and FX rate at which the investor does the one-time conversion from home to base currency before buying the DCI is just as important as the terms of the DCI itself.

(b) What is the right size to invest in a DCI?

To answer this question, we need to know if the investor has a real need for the alternate currency.

If the investor has a real need for the underlying alternate currency, the size of the DCI is ideally highly related to the need for that currency. For example, if he is thinking that he may have some need for UK Pounds to finance his child's undergraduate studies in London, he may need say £18,000 a year in fees plus another £20,000 in living expenses per year. So he may want to consider a DCI of £38,000, or about US$59,000. He could consider an amount that is a multiple of that if he chooses to finance the entire three to five years of undergraduate studies upfront. However, a DCI amount of say US$500,000 would certainly over-hedge the underlying need, and move into the next section of discussion.

If the investor does *not* have a real need for the underlying alternate currency, we can assume that he is trying to express a view on the underlying currencies, while hoping to enhance his return via the selling of "volatility". In this case, the right size is what the investor would be comfortable to stomach in terms of losses. A word of caution is that unlike stocks, "fundamental valuation" of a currency is not as clear-cut or easy. To me, FX is an easy-to-understand instrument, but arguably the most difficult to master. Plan for up to 20% losses – that would be my conservative advice. For example,

DCI – Best and worst outcomes if your view is right

Typical structure where you are delivered the alternate currency if it weakens beyond the strike price on maturity. Strike is typically set 1–1.5% weaker than the current FX spot level for short-dated (up to 1 month) DCIs.

Your view of the alternate currency at maturity	You have an underlying need for the alternate currency	You do NOT have an underlying need for the alternate currency
Bearish ↘	**Best:** Paid high yield, spot is right around your strike at maturity **Worst:** Alternate currency delivered, and its spot is much weaker than strike **Do it if...** yield is high or you really want the alternate currency at the strike price because you are likely to be delivered if your bearish view is right!	**Best:** Paid high yield, alternate currency not delivered **Worst:** Alternate currency delivered, and its spot is much weaker than strike **Do it if...** yield is high or you think the alternate currency will trade only slightly weaker AND you don't mind owning the alternate currency for trading purposes even if delivered
Sideways →	**Best:** Paid high yield, alternate currency is slightly weaker **Worst:** Alternate currency is slightly stronger, so you will have to pay more to buy it **Do it if...** you think the FX is just going to be moving sideways and you don't mind buying the alternate currency even if slightly stronger than current spot FX level	**Best:** Paid high yield **Worst:** None **Do it if...** you think the FX is just going to be moving sideways; this is perfect for DCI!
Bullish ↗	**Best:** Paid high yield, alternate currency is only slightly stronger **Worst:** Alternate currency is much stronger, and you will have to pay much more to buy it **Do it if...** *only if* yield is crazy high because you are much better off just buying the alternate currency now instead!	**Best:** Paid high yield **Worst:** None **Do it if...** yield is high or you are only mildly bullish on the alternate currency, as you may be better off just buying the alternate currency now for trading instead

HIGH NET WORTH INVESTING

if you think you could afford to lose US$20,000, then a DCI amount of US$100,000 might be a starting point.

Conclusion

The risks and rewards of DCI are fairly clear and observable. In my view, DCI is most suited to an investor who has an underlying need for the alternate currency (or even base currency, if different from the home currency). There is nothing worse than having more of the alternate currency than you need and be forced to take a loss by converting it back to another base or your home currency.

For an investor who does not have an underlying need for the alternate currency, DCI is one way for him to express his view on FX by selling volatility. If the investor is not active in the FX market, this is an acceptable investment route. If investor is very active in FX and sophisticated, he should consider going through the direct route of opening an FX trading account with the bank or a dedicated online FX trading portal, trading FX Spot, Forwards and Options directly.

CHAPTER 7

Structured Deposits

A Structured Deposit (SD for short), as the name implies, is a deposit with a structure around it. It is a way for investors to earn a higher deposit rate by expressing a view on one or more linked asset classes, like commodities, FX or equities. If the view turns out right, the investor will earn the higher interest. If the view is wrong, the investor typically gets back the principal with no interest.

In most countries, SDs sold are principal-protected. However, some countries do have non-principal-protected structured deposits. These are used by more aggressive investors, where they choose to get back less than their starting principal if their views turn out wrong, in exchange for higher interest rates if they are right. In this case, the use of the word "deposit" may be a misnomer, as one usually wouldn't expect to lose one's principal in a deposit. As such, I would prefer to call these Structured Notes or Structured Investments. To avoid any confusion, this chapter only covers principal-protected structured deposits. Non-principal-protected structures like currency-linked structured investments/notes are covered in other chapters.

A structured deposit is typically a deposit with a linked derivative, whose return depends on the performance of the underlying asset. Banks can structure an SD based on an investor's unique needs, and it typically starts as low as $10,000, with tenure ranging typically from one month and up.

Given their flexibility, SDs can be used by investors to earn a higher interest return, manage their cash flows, or express a view in a cheap way that doesn't cost them any capital. What buyers of principal-protected SDs are doing is essentially "investing" the interest they would be earning from the principal placed with the bank to express a view. If they are right, they would be rewarded, as any right investments would. If their views are wrong, they forego the interest they would have otherwise earned for the period.

It is not possible to cover all the different types of SDs in the market here as the permutations are numerous. However, they are usually variations of the following few – "betting" that an underlying asset will either trade higher, trade lower, or trade in a range in a specified tenure.

There are various names accorded by different institutions for similar SDs. The names are not really important; what is important is that the investor needs to have a view, understand the structure, and be happy with the corresponding return and risk characteristics.

Common Variations of SDs

Below we look at three examples: a European Digital SD linked to Gold; a Range Accrual SD linked to the US S&P 500 stock index; and a Tiered Tower Deposit linked to USD/JPY FX.

European Digital SD Linked to Gold	
Underlying Asset	Gold (XAU/USD) spot
Base Currency	USD
Tenure	3 months
Current Spot	1200
Strike	1095
Interest Rate	5%
Scenarios	
(a) At maturity, if underlying asset is at or below the strike…	Investor receives principal + interest based on the agreed Interest Rate
(b) At maturity, if underlying asset is above the strike…	Investor receives principal only

The above is an example of how an investor could express a bearish view on Gold. Similarly, if the investor is bullish, the strike could simply be set at a higher level.

Range Accrual SD Linked to US S&P 500 Stock Index	
Underlying Asset	US S&P 500 stock index
Base Currency	USD
Tenure	6 months
Current Spot	2100
Range	1900–2300
Interest Rate	6%
Scenarios	
(a) During the entire tenure of the SD, every day the underlying asset stays within the range…	Investor earns the agreed Interest Rate for that day
(b) During the entire tenure of the SD, every day the underlying asset stays outside the range…	Investor earns no interest
(c) On maturity	Investor gets principal + the accumulated interest earned based on the two scenarios above

This is an example of how an investor could express a range view on US stocks. In this range accrual example, the investor is probably not entirely certain that the stocks will not trade temporarily outside the range specified, but is broadly certain that the range is where the stocks will be trading for the majority of the SD tenure.

Tiered Tower Deposit Linked to USD/JPY FX	
Underlying Asset	USD/JPY FX Spot
Base Currency	USD
Tenure	4 months
Current Spot	111
Range 1	108–114
Range 2	105–117
Interest Rate 1	8%
Interest Rate 2	4%
Scenarios	
(a) If underlying asset trades within Range 1 for the entire tenure…	Investor receives principal + interest based on the agreed Interest Rate 1
(b) If underlying asset trades wider than Range 1 but stays within Range 2 for the entire tenure…	Investor receives principal + interest based on the agreed Interest Rate 2
(c) If underlying asset trades wider than Range 2 during the tenure…	Investor receives principal only

This is an example of how an investor could express a range view on USD/JPY FX. In this tower deposit example, the investor is reasonably certain that the USD/JPY FX will not trade outside the larger Range 2. If USD/JPY trades in the narrower Range 1 during the tenure, so much the better as he would earn the higher interest rate.

How to Design a Structured Deposit?

Before you rush out now to do an SD to enhance your yield, ask yourself whether you know the best structure to express your view? If you answer yes, then you are probably a seasoned investor familiar with financial instrument structuring. Most of you would probably answer no, in which case it is best to speak with your Relationship Manager (RM) for advice. Share the following with your RM:

- The specific asset class you have a view on

- The tenure for your view playing out

- How strong your conviction is with regard to your view

- Whether you are prepared to lose part of your principal if you are wrong

Based on the above, your RM will be able to advise you on the best way to express your view. The fourth point is important, because if you are prepared to lose part of your principal, then the structure your RM may propose may be one of Structured Investment or Structured Note, where your principal is at risk. If you are not prepared to lose any part of your principal at all, then an SD could follow.

Next, evaluate if the structured deposit proposed accurately reflects your view, and whether the interest rate offered justifies the risks that you will be taking. Do not be afraid to adjust your strikes or ranges until you achieve a risk-reward level that you are comfortable with. Feel free to compare prices across different banks too if you have banking relationships with more than one bank.

Why Invest in Structured Deposits?

SDs are most used by relatively conservative investors who want to enhance the yield they receive on their cash. They would most likely compare the returns of an SD to a Time Deposit (Fixed Deposit). They do not want to take too much risk and are not prepared to put their capital at risk, but are willing to risk their potential traditional deposit interest income in exchange for a potentially higher return.

If you are a seasoned investor familiar with financial products, this may not be for you. You could replicate that by expressing your views directly through financial products and derivatives like FX Options, while putting your cash in a traditional deposit product. The end result is the same, except with slightly lower costs.

SD has a place in most retail investors' portfolio because most retail investors are either not too sophisticated, or do not have that much capital to trade directly in the underlying financial product or derivative due to large trading size requirements. For example, one would typically need to trade at least $100,000 in notional value for an FX Option with a bank. When used wisely, SD can certainly occupy a small portion in one's overall asset allocation.

Other Considerations Before Investing in Structured Deposits

Like a Time Deposit, a Structured Deposit definitely returns the investor minimally the principal on maturity. If the SD has to be terminated before maturity, the investor may not get the full principal back, as early termination of an SD involves unwinding the underlying financial derivative. Irrespective of whether one's view of the underlying asset has been right or wrong up till the point of early termination, it seldom makes sense to early terminate as the transaction and administrative costs charged by the institution to unwind the underlying derivative almost always cost more than the accrued interests or value up to that point. In the best case, one would only get back one's principal in full, if the market is in the investor's favour.

Most investors should only invest in SDs in their own base currency. If one has to buy a foreign currency just for the purpose of the structured deposit, one has to be cognisant of the FX risks associated. As SD is not a very high-yielding investment product – typically yielding in the mid-single digit percentage (on an annualised basis) – it would normally not make sense once the FX risk is factored in. The FX conversion risk at maturity could more than wipe out any potential returns from the SD, and so exposes the investor to the potential of capital loss.

Conclusion

Despite the many variations of structured deposits available in the markets, SD is really a simple and safe investment product. It could be used to enhance an investor's yield on cash, without putting any capital at risk, while only risking the potential interest return. Given the ease in structuring an SD, it certainly has a place in most retail investors' portfolios. Investors could consider a combination of SDs and other cash products in managing the liquid cash in their portfolio.

CHAPTER 8

Unit Trusts

A UNIT TRUST is essentially a sum of money managed collectively by a professional fund manager. An investor who buys into units in a unit trust will have his money pooled with that of other investors and invested in one or more selected asset classes in order to achieve the stated investment objective. A unit trust is sometimes also called a Collective Investment Scheme, or sometimes simply a fund for short.

There are hundreds of different unit trusts in the market. Each of them may invest in a different asset, or a combination of assets. They are also invested in different markets, with different investment objectives. Their investment objectives will usually clearly state what asset classes they are investing in, their investment strategy or time horizon, and what their benchmarks are.

There are unit trusts which invest in macro themes, as well as those which invest in very narrow themes, like the pharmaceutical sector, for instance. Some invest in a single country bond market, some invest in regional or global corporate and government bonds. Some invest in currency or cash and cash equivalent products, some invest in properties.

Some are actively managed unit trusts whose aim is to beat their benchmark return. Some are passively managed by merely replicating the benchmark. Essentially, there are likely to be unit trusts out there that would suit everyone's unique needs.

It is not easy to classify the risk rating of each unit trust based only on their investment asset types, or on their investment markets/countries, as there are too many variables. When assessing the risk, one should broadly consider the following:

◆ Broad asset class (e.g. bonds, equities, cash)

◆ Countries of investment (e.g. single country vs regional/global)

◆ Instruments used (e.g. vanilla products or derivatives)

◆ Sub asset class (if applicable; e.g. corporate bonds vs government bonds)

◆ Leverage (i.e. is any leverage used?)

The diagram below provides a sense of the potential risk and return profiles of different types of unit trusts. Note that it is for general guidance only. Bond unit trusts that focus on emerging market government bonds or high-yield corporate bonds may not necessarily be safer than unit trusts that invest in "blue chip" equities. This is because high-yield corporate bonds may expose the fund to significant credit risks.

Potential Risk and Return	Type of Unit Trust
High	• Narrowly focused/specialised unit trust • Leveraged unit trust
Medium	• Balanced unit trust invested in all asset classes
Low	• Bond unit trust • Money market unit trust

What is the Difference Between Unit Trusts and Mutual Funds?

Like unit trusts, mutual funds are also investment schemes that pool investors' money together and manage it professionally. Mutual funds started in the US, and are very similar to unit trusts. The little differences lie in the legal structure, and may vary from country to country. Strategy-wise, they are almost identical, and many refer to unit trusts as mutual funds and vice versa.

How to Choose a Unit Trust?

As there are so many unit trusts out there in the market, how does an investor decide on which to choose? There are several considerations one should think about, in the following order:

◈ Your investment objective and time horizon

◈ Types of unit trusts that fit into the above, and your risk appetite

❖ Pick the "best" unit trusts matching your strategy

❖ Review periodically the unit trusts' performance to ensure adherence to your strategy

(a) Your investment objective and time horizon

Broadly, an investor should consider whether to invest for income, retirement, capital gains, etc., and consider how long they could afford to stay invested in the strategy. In general, unit trust is more suitable for an investor with a longer investment time horizon (>1 year) as the transaction costs involved are quite high and therefore it does not make sense to be trading or speculating in them for the short term.

(b) Types of unit trusts that fit into the above, and your risk appetite

Once you have defined your investment objective and horizon, you can start picking the types of unit trusts that fit your strategy and risk appetite. For example, if you are young and your investment objective is for capital gains in the long term (>5 years) with no short-term income needs, then an equity fund with a growth focus may be suitable for you.

If you are a relatively conservative investor and find that you want exposure to bonds, a bond unit trust may be ideal as the fund manager would have a diversified portfolio of bonds which a retail investor would not be able to achieve with a small sum of money.

If you are of the view that stocks and bonds are over-valued in the near term, you might want to place your money in a money market unit trust, while waiting for the best time to switch back into a bond or equity unit trust.

(c) Pick the "best" unit trusts matching your strategy

Now you can start checking the market to see what's available that meets your needs. How do you pick the "best" unit trusts that match your strategy? What is "best" anyway?

All unit trusts come with the warning that "past performance is not indicative of future performance". That obviously does not stop an investor from comparing the performance of comparable unit trusts. Some investors may find comfort in those that have done better relative to others in the recent past. Others may believe in "reversion to the mean" and choose trusted fund managers with good "pedigree" who are therefore likely to outperform in the near future after a relatively poor recent run. There is no right or wrong in unit trust selection, and a lot depends on an investor's risk appetite and confidence in the fund manager.

What is more objective and thus comparable might be the fees charged by the fund house, which are as follows:

⬥ Management Fee: A unit trust, like a fund, is managed by professional fund managers. The fund managers are paid to manage the money. This "pay" comes from the management fee that the unit trust charges, typically 0.5–2%. This is the main fee charged by the unit trust manager.

⬥ Trustee Fee: This is an annual fee charged by the trustee for the provision of custody services for safekeeping the fund's assets. This usually ranges from 0.1% to 0.15%.

❖ Other Fees: There may be other fees charged too, like an administrative fee, audit fee, etc. These are typically not large when compared against the management fee.

While most data on funds' financial performance is already net of fees, it is still worthwhile for an investor to know what fees a manager charges as these are fixed costs, irrespective of how the manager performs, and would matter greatly especially for passively managed funds. To help compare across unit trusts, most times we could look for the published Expense Ratio of a unit trust. This is the ratio of its operating expense to the average value of its assets under management (AUM). As operating expense is taken out of the unit trust's assets, a high expense ratio implies a high cost to running the unit trust, and reduces the return to the investment. As such, a quick comparison of Expense Ratios across different unit trusts would give a quick indication of the relative costs of running each of them.

Besides fees charged by the fund, there are charges by the distributor of the unit trusts too. They are:

❖ Sales Charge: Investors tend to buy their unit trusts through banks or investment intermediaries or online investment portals. There is a cost involved for these agencies to sell the unit trusts, and they recoup that cost via the Sales Charge. This sales charge is sometimes called a "front-end load". It ranges from 0.1% to as much as 5%, so an investor would do well to shop around for the lowest rate.

◆ Redemption Fee: Some unit trusts charge investors a fee at the point of selling. This is sometimes called a "back-end load". Usually those agencies that charge a hefty upfront sales charge have no selling redemption fee, but this is by no means a certainty. Some unit trusts "reward" investors for holding on to the trust for long periods and have a declining scale for the redemption fee, sometimes down to zero if the unit trust has been held for more than say three years.

◆ Switching Fee: Most fund houses manage a variety of unit trusts under them. If an investor chooses to switch out of one unit trust to another unit trust under the same fund house, they usually do not have to pay the redemption fee and the sales charge, but just pay a Switching Fee. This fee is sort of an incentive to the investor to stay with the same fund manager. The fee is typically less than 1%.

(d) Review periodically the unit trusts' performance to ensure adherence to your strategy

Your work is not done when you have picked your unit trusts and invested in them. As unit trusts are not managed by yourself directly, that usually means you should spend more time reviewing their performance periodically to ensure that the performance is what you expected. A unit trust should ideally be performing in line with your expectations of the asset class/strategy. If there are unusual large drawdowns inconsistent with the investment objective, one should be extra cautious and do the necessary further due diligence to decide if one should stay on with the unit trust.

Changes to unit trust selection should be kept minimal to avoid the high transaction costs that come with it. Unit trusts are not like single-stock investment, so some patience with them is advised. When there are major changes to the key portfolio managers managing the funds, or when you change your investment allocation or strategy, it is an opportune time to review the composition of your holdings of unit trusts and assess whether to hold on to them.

Why Invest in Unit Trusts?

Most investors consider unit trust investment because of one or more of the following reasons:

(1) Don't know how to invest directly in a particular asset class – they are usually novice investors who do not have much investment experience.

(2) "Too much work" to invest directly – they are usually busy professionals who just cannot be bothered or have no time to "stock pick".

(3) Don't have enough capital to invest in that asset class – they are usually somewhat investment-savvy people who want exposure to a certain asset class like bonds but realise that their intended

investment capital may be too small to get in or too small to be well diversified within that asset class.

(4) No access to an underlying asset class – they are usually experienced investors who want access to a particular "closed" investment asset/country. They will source out the right unit trusts that have the desired access, for example through on-shore presence.

(5) Prefer professional managers – they could range from novice investors to veteran investors who simply think that the professional fund managers are likely to do a better job than themselves.

We have discussed that before investing, we must think about our investment objective, investment horizon, investment strategy, and consider cost and performance in picking a unit trust. The most important question you should ask yourself before investing in unit trusts is: Can I do a better job myself than investing in the unit trust?

If your reason for investing in unit trusts is one of reasons (1) or (2) or (5), and you fully intend to stay that way, go ahead and invest in the chosen unit trusts.

If your reason is (3), have you considered other investment avenues? For example, if you are keen to gain exposure to Hong Kong stocks, have you considered investing in an Exchange-Traded Fund (ETF) linked to the Hang Seng Index for example?

If your reason is (4), you have probably considered alternatives and I have little to add, except that you should consider how a sudden closure of that market might impact your investment strategy and cash flows. In that scenario, as has happened occasionally to emerging markets, your capital may be stuck and you can't liquidate your investments.

Other Considerations Before Investing in Unit Trusts

One very often overlooked criterion in unit trust selection is the currency exposure. There is obviously FX risk to the investor if he invests in a unit trust that is denominated in a different currency from his home currency. If the investor invests in a unit trust denominated in the same currency as his home currency, then surely there is no FX risk? Is that true? What if the unit trust invests in foreign assets – is FX risk still relevant to the investor?

When a unit trust invests in a foreign asset but prices the unit trust in a different base currency, there is FX risk. The only time there is no direct FX risk in the unit trust is when the manager only invests in assets that are in the same currency as the unit trust. FX risks are often the most over-looked by both fund managers and investors. Fund managers usually care much more about the local currency returns, and tend to leave the base currency or more often than not the USD return to "someone else" to deal with. Some fund managers have dedicated FX managers to handle the FX hedging on behalf of all funds or unit trusts under the fund house, while others may just leave the currency exposure unhedged, arguing that currencies tend to be mean-reverting in the long run. Depending on the underlying FX movements of the base currency versus the invested currencies, there could be large differences in performance returns. Let's look at a simplified example of a unit trust with no FX hedging:

> In July 2014, a USD-based investor buys into a USD-denominated unit trust that has a mandate of beating the returns of the benchmark Japanese equity index of the Nikkei 225. The US Dollar to Japanese Yen FX (USD/JPY) is at 100 and the Nikkei 225 index is at 15,620. One year later, in July 2015, the Nikkei 225 index has gone up to 20,585, an increase of a whopping 31.8%. Let's assume the unit trust did just as well as the Nikkei 225.

In local currency, i.e. Yen terms, the unit trust's gain is about 31.8%. If the investor wants to redeem his investment now, how much did he make? In July 2015, USD/JPY was at about 123, i.e. JPY depreciated about 23% in the same period. As the unit trust is priced in USD, the fund manager would in theory have to convert the value of the investment from Yen into USD before returning the money to the investor. The investor gets back his investment in USD, and finds that his profit in USD terms is just above 7%, no thanks to the weaker Yen. So the unit trust investor thought that he was not exposed to FX risk because his base is USD and he bought a USD unit trust. But his USD returns are only 7% even though he got the view of rallying Japanese equities right! If the unit trust had a hedging policy and had hedged its currency risks correctly, the USD return would be better than 7%.

What this example goes to show is that the hedging policy adopted by a unit trust is an important consideration when choosing a unit trust too. It also highlights that an investor is exposed to FX risk as soon as he buys into a unit trust that is invested in foreign assets. He is exposed even when he buys a unit trust with a base currency similar to his "home currency" because the unit trust may be investing in foreign assets.

Conclusion

Investing in unit trusts, or mutual funds as they are called in some jurisdictions, is something that appears simple but isn't. Due to the large selection of unit trusts available in the market, it is sometimes mind-boggling to know which to pick. If we go into selection without a clear idea of our investment strategy, we are likely to be sub-optimal in our selection. Due to the relatively high transaction costs, mistakes are very costly. One should always know why one is involved in unit trusts, and not regret later due to high cost, poor performance, or simply wrong strategy.

Unit trusts provide a quick and simple way to participate in the performance of a selected strategy, so they are popular among novice investors. Veteran investors use unit trusts to their advantage by selecting those with managers they perceive as good or those that provide access to assets or countries they otherwise could not get into. One of the key considerations that is often forgotten is the FX exposure. This can sometimes be the key differentiator between a good unit trust and an outstanding one.

CHAPTER 9

Insurance

INSURANCE IS A RATHER unpopular word in some parts of the world. It is almost taboo for some of the older generation to even talk about it, for it is usually associated with death or unlucky events like injury, hospitalisation, etc. The good news is that increasingly, as the education level of the general population is raised globally, the understanding and acceptance of insurance is gaining traction, particularly in Asian societies.

Insurance is the practice of providing protection against a particular event, which may or may not be related to human life or well-being. Besides the usual insurance against human life and property, insurance can now be bought to protect against default by a corporate's debt or product, or simply any asset that has a tangible value. For example, a Credit Default Swap (CDS) is a product traded in the financial markets to protect against a default by a particular country or firm issuing debt. Strictly speaking, it is not an insurance product, but it does function similarly because the buyer pays a premium and in return receives a payout if a specific adverse event occurs.

For the purpose of this chapter, we will focus only on products that are normally used by a retail investor relating to life insurance and investment products linked to life insurance, mainly from the investment and legacy planning perspective. It will exclude discussions on medical insurance, total and permanent disability (TPD) coverage, home insurance, travel insurance, car insurance, etc.

Types of Life Insurance Products

The common types of life insurance products include:

- Whole Life Policy
- Term (Life) Policy
- Endowment Policy
- Investment-Linked Policy
- Universal Life Policy

All of the above policies have a payout when the insured passes away. Other than Term Policy, those with a fixed maturity date are often used as a forced savings plan while doubling up as an insurance policy should the insured not survive to the maturity date. For those that only pay out upon the death of the insured, they are usually used for legacy planning, to benefit dependants or loved ones. It is worth mentioning that the person paying the insurance premium need not be the same person as the insured, though most insurance underwriters would like to see a relationship between the two.

Each of the above types has its own unique characteristics meant to suit different needs. There are also minor variations between different insurers, and one can further customise them by having "riders" and other options over-laid. The most common riders include Critical Illness and Total and Permanent Disability coverage. Medical coverage is clearly important, with rising healthcare costs globally, so a policy with such coverage added would not come cheap.

For our purposes, what's important is to understand the core product types, so we will focus here on the key charac-teristics of each of them.

(a) Whole Life Policy

This is probably the most common policy bought by people looking for protection against death. The structure is straightforward. One pays a monthly, quarterly or annual premium for either a fixed number of years or until death, and in exchange the insurance policy pays out a "death bene-fit" upon one's death.

The policy accumulates a "cash value" from the fourth year typically, which can be cashed out if one decides to ter-minate the policy. Sometimes one may prefer to keep the policy, but may be in need of cash for an emergency. In that case, one could borrow against the policy's cash value at a rate generally better than borrowing from a bank. Alternatively, if the policy is "paid up", one could also use the accumulated cash value to help pay the insurance premium for the policy in later years instead of using one's own cash then.

For most whole life policies, the cash value would only exceed the total premium paid up from the 12th to 15th years onwards. There is no cash value in the first three policy years because the expenses, distribution and sales cost for a life policy are rather high, and that basically is covered by a good part of the first three years of premium paid. Most life policies only start to generate a decent return from the 15th year onwards, as the policies take time to recover from the first three years of negative cash values. Thus, the longer one contributes and holds on to a life policy, the more likely one would get a higher annualised return over the entire period. Put another way, one should not use it as a savings tool if one does not intend to hold on to the policy for the very long term.

If a life policy is still in force when the insured passes away, the death benefit will accrue to the named beneficiaries. As such, whole life policies are generally used for creating an estate.

(b) Term (Life) Policy

As its name implies, a term policy (or term life policy as it relates to life insurance) is in force for a fixed term. This term could typically be 10, 15, 20, 25 or 30 years. If the insured lives beyond the fixed term, there will be no payout to the named beneficiaries. This fixed term feature is the biggest difference with a whole life policy.

The second key difference is that term policy is a lot cheaper than whole life policy because it does not accumulate any cash value. As such, term policy is a cheap and efficient way to protect one's life or "earning potential". It is useful when one is young, can't afford to pay the high premium of a whole life policy or has other competing needs for cash, but still needs to insure one's life to ensure loved ones are provided for should the unfortunate happen.

The logical question to ask next is, if you could afford a whole life policy's premium, should you buy a whole life policy or buy a term life policy and invest the premium difference by yourself? The answer depends on two things – the return generated by the insurer's investment team, versus the return generated by your own investment. We established earlier that the annualised returns improve over time for a whole life policy. That means the shorter your intended investment term, the better for you to invest by yourself. There are many studies comparing the two, and obviously this is fraught with difficulty as the two sets of return numbers vary. As a very rough guide, a life policy typically generates a return in excess of 4% if held for 20 years or more. That means if you were to invest by yourself and your investment horizon is 20 years, then you need to beat this 4% return number annually for it to be worth your while to do it yourself.

(c) Endowment Policy

An endowment plan is a fixed term regular savings and investment life policy. It usually stipulates the guaranteed and non-guaranteed returns over the tenure of the policy, and the policy pays out on maturity or on death, whichever comes first. Typical tenures range from 10 years to 30 years. An endowment policy can be thought of as a forced savings plan that offers an element of life protection.

The most common type of endowment is the With-Profit Endowment, where regular bonuses or reversionary bonuses are declared at intervals and guaranteed at maturity, and there is also a non-guaranteed bonus at maturity called the terminal bonus to encourage policy holders to hold to maturity.

Due to the savings nature of an endowment policy, it is usually used when one is saving for a particular purpose. For example, some may buy an 18-year endowment plan at their child's birth as a form of savings to provide for their child's overseas college education. If the insured unfortunately passes away before that, the education fund for the child is provided for from the death benefit that the policy would pay.

Typically, endowment policies do not invest in high-risk products, and so their terminal value policy tends to be more stable, assuming of course no serious adverse market disruptions. The rate of return varies with the tenure – the longer one is able to hold on to the policy, the higher the expected rate of return. The reason for this is similar to what was described under Whole Life Policy, where some time is needed to recover from the costs and expenses linked to selling the policy. The actual rate of return depends on market conditions as well as the capability of the fund manager. The return profile is also quite similar to a Whole Life Policy, so generally speaking, one can expect to start having a decent rate of return from the 15th year on.

The main difference between an endowment and a whole life policy is in the number of years of premium contribution as well as the amount. Due to the shorter number of years of premium payment, to achieve a similar amount of death benefit, the dollar amount contribution is much higher in an endowment policy.

(d) Investment-Linked Policy

There are many names for an Investment-Linked Policy, sometimes called ILP for short. Other common names include Investment-Linked Insurance Plan or Unit-Linked Insurance Plan (ULIP). What is common between them is that they are made up of an insurance plan and the option to invest in a variety of asset classes such as stocks, bonds and money market funds. There is a large variety of ILPs in the market as they can be easily tailor-made to suit different needs. More common variants include single premium versus regular premiums, fixed term versus life, choice of investment products and the ability to switch between a pre-determined set of funds.

An ILP is very similar to an Endowment Policy. The line is increasingly blurred over the years as people get more sophisticated and demand more choices. Broadly, the key difference between them is the ability of ILP holders to decide what to invest in, and when. So an ILP policy holder will start with investments in one or more funds managed by the insurer, and can choose to vary these investments when he deems fit. For example, when the insured is younger, he may choose to invest 80% in an equity fund, and 20% in a bond fund. When he is older, he may gradually shift more into bonds. Shifts within funds managed by the insurer typically carry little to no costs, and so this is an attractive way to express one's investment views while saving, and having life coverage at the same time.

(e) Universal Life Policy

Universal Life Insurance, or UL for short, is a variation of Whole Life Insurance. The key feature is the flexibility for the buyer to decide on the premium amount, the cash value, and the insurance coverage amount. It can sometimes be adjusted during the life of the policy to suit the buyer's needs. Cost of insurance and other fees are deducted from the premium monthly, interest on the cash value accrued will then be credited to the account. This interest is subject to a minimum rate as contracted, typically 2% currently (from 4% in the 1980s), though there is a distinct possibility of that going even lower due to the low interest rate environment we have been in. Note, however, that even 2% interest does not guarantee that the cash value of the policy will continue to grow, as the cost of insurance and fees may be more than this minimum rate. A key difference between UL and Whole Life Policy is that the holder can use the interest earned to help pay premiums.

Universal Life Insurance has evolved over time. When it was first mooted, it was popular due to its preferential tax treatment on the interest paid in the policy. This benefit has dwindled over time, and varies from country to country.

There are single premium UL and regular premium UL plans. Single premium UL has generally been more popular in recent years due to the leverage one can have from borrowing to buy the policy. For example, a UL policy for a 45-year-old male might cost $300,000 for $1 million coverage. Instead of forking out the $300,000 upfront, he can borrow say 70% or $210,000 to finance this UL purchase, pledging the policy to the financier. He would typically only need to finance the interest of this loan instead of interest plus principal. With this financing feature, he effectively would have $1 million insurance coverage with $90,000 premium paid upfront, a leverage of more than 10 times. When he passes away, the insurance company will first pay the amount owed to the financier, and then pay the balance to the beneficiaries. In

	Whole Life Policy	Term Policy
Insurance Premium	Constant	Low and Constant or premiums start low and increase at renewal with age, but renewal is not guaranteed
Years of Coverage	For life, capped at 100 typically	For fixed term, usually renewable until at least official retirement age
Choice of Investment Funds	No; decided by the Insurer	Not applicable
Death Benefit	Minimum guaranteed; varies relative to investment returns of insurance company (participating plan)	Guaranteed; may be increased or decreased by policy holder
Cash Value	Minimum guaranteed; fluctuates with underlying investment performance	None
Cash Value Growth	Insurer determines guaranteed cash value and declares dividends based on performance of its investment portfolio	No cash value

Endowment Policy	Investment-Linked Policy	Universal Life Policy
Constant	Single or Constant or could be increased or decreased by policy holder	Single, or Flexible; absolute amount is high as minimum coverage tends to be high
For fixed term	Fixed term or for life (100 typically)	For life, capped at 121 typically
No; decided by the Insurer	Yes	Policy holder decides between Traditional Bond & Equity-linked at inception; no changes thereafter
Minimum guaranteed; varies relative to investment returns of insurance company (participating plan)	Guaranteed typically at Net Asset Value or 105% of premium paid, whichever is higher	May not be guaranteed due to cash value fluctuations; varies relative to investment returns
Minimum guaranteed; fluctuates with underlying investment performance	Fluctuates with chosen investment funds' performance	Guaranteed minimum interest rate typically; fluctuates with underlying investment performance
Insurer determines guaranteed cash value and declares dividends based on performance of its investment portfolio	Cash value growth depends on the investment performance of your chosen funds	Insurer determines cash value interest crediting rates based on interest rate returns to the company

this case, assuming the death benefit remains constant at $1 million, the beneficiaries could expect to receive $790,000, which is still a good 8.8 times the initial premium paid.

Given the high leverage one can achieve from UL, UL tends to be a tool used by the wealthy or high net worth individuals for estate planning. With the flexibility of UL, it is sometimes also used as an alternative investment. The reason it is mainly only used by the wealthy is that the minimum insured amount for UL tends to be high, typically from $500,000, putting it out of reach for most men on the street.

Which Life Insurance Policy Meets Your Needs?

Now that we have covered the various common types of life insurance, which type should you pick? The answer obviously depends on what your needs are and what you intend the policy for. These are some of the questions you should ask yourself:

- ◆ What is your insurance/investment objective?

- ◆ What is your investment/insurance time horizon?

- ◆ Which insurance policies really fit the above, and your risk appetite?

Once you have answered the above questions, you will then be better placed to pick the right insurance policy out there matching your strategy and needs.

Your Insurance/Investment Objective?

This question appears trivial but is not. Ask yourself if you are looking at insurance mainly to provide a protection on your life or if you are after the investment return that comes with a life policy, or a combination. Here are three possible answers:

(a) Protection on your life only; no other investment objective

If this is your answer, then the solution is straightforward. Just buy a Term Policy. It is inexpensive premium-wise, and will provide you the maximum insurance per dollar of premium you pay.

(b) Protection on your life and investment return

This is where you might have to think a lot harder and decide what type of insurance policies suit you better. It depends to a large extent on how much premium you are willing to contribute on a regular basis, how active you would like to be managing your investment portfolio, and how much flexibility you need. Refer to the table on page 170–171 for a comparison between the different types of insurance policies and you should be able to narrow down your choices.

Very broadly, if you are young and starting out your career without much cash to spare, a Whole Life Policy or Endowment Policy may be your choice. If you have investment experience and are keen to express your investment views, an Investment-Linked Policy may suit you. If you are slightly older, financially secure, and thinking of financial planning and estate planning, a Universal Life Policy is probably the choice.

(c) Investment return only

If this is your only objective without the need for a life protection element, then you should perhaps look elsewhere. While some insurance companies do provide almost pure investment or savings policies like an Endowment Policy, they still tend to come with hefty sales commissions, high distribution fees and other costs. This makes the return in the first few years of the policy relatively poor as compared to other pure investment products like unit trusts or ETFs. If you are still not deterred, then scrutinise the guaranteed (if any) and non-guaranteed return numbers offered by the insurance company very carefully before taking the plunge.

Your Investment/Insurance Time Horizon?

This question is closely linked to the earlier question on your objective. Again, here are three possible answers:

(a) Short Term (<12 years)

A Term Policy might be the best choice. This is almost independent of what your investment/insurance objective may be, and the reason is simple. For such a "short" term (from the insurance perspective), if the objective is for investment returns, then insurance products are really quite a bad choice. The reason is that typical policies with cash values only break even some time between the 12th and 15th policy year, due to the high distribution costs and fees charged in the first three policy years. As such, if you have such a short time horizon, you are better off sticking with one without cash value, i.e. a Term Policy.

(b) Long Term (>12 years up to 30 years)

Here you are open to all the different types of life policies available, including even Whole Life Policy and Universal Life Policy. The reason they are suitable is that they accumulate cash value in the life of the policy, and provide the option of early termination if you should need it. If at inception you think that there is a good chance that you might terminate a Whole Life or Universal Life policy early, please carefully consider the cost and penalty (if any) of doing so, and also compare the guaranteed and unguaranteed portions of the cash value projections with those fixed term policies. As the policy statement usually states, life policies are long-term commitment, so please enter the contract with care!

(c) For Life

Clearly Whole Life and Universal Life policies are applicable. For some insurance companies, Investment-Linked Policies may also have the whole life tenure option. Typically, if this is your insurance/investment time horizon, you are not thinking of benefiting yourself but buying this policy as a form of legacy and estate planning to benefit your dependants or next generation. As such, the most important consideration besides the projected investment returns would be the reliability and credibility of the insurance company. You don't want to invest in a company that may not outlive you!

Which Insurance Policies Really Fit the Above and Your Risk Appetite?

With clear answers from above, you are now ready to narrow your choices down to probably one or two types of insurance. There are many insurance companies out there offering variations of the generic types of insurance you may be after. As each of them may be slightly different, that makes comparison a little challenging. Most policies do come with illustrations using standardised maximum rates of return typically legislated by insurance watchdogs. They obviously do not mean that the policies will generate that return, but this standard return rate is helpful in facilitating comparison across policies from different companies. Policies with slightly different features and add-ons would however make the comparison complex, and further complicate your decision making process. This is when you need to be clear with your own risk appetite, and the following points may help:

- ◆ Ask for recent investment return numbers from the insurance company, and you can make a judgement on whether they are likely to continue delivering similar performances going forward.

- ◆ If the projected return numbers going forward are similar, you can compare the guaranteed cash value of the policies over time. This will give a clear indication of how much the cost of insurance and fees are for each insurer.

◆ If you think you may early terminate a policy, it is important to compare the guaranteed and non-guaranteed cash value for that year (say in 15–20 years' time) to understand if there are any potential big jumps in cash value after a certain year, which is a feature offered by some insurers to reward loyalty. It is important too to ask if there is any penalty for early withdrawal or redemption.

◆ Compare the premium amounts to see how you could get the best bang for your buck in terms of insured amount and investment returns.

◆ Do not be distracted by all the bells and whistles that may be present unless they are really important to you. Remember to focus on the key points – insured amount, tenure, premium and returns (cash value). Everything else should be secondary to them.

At the end of the day, after all your research and comparison, you are likely to narrow your options down to one or two products. One last recommendation I would make, which may be one of the most important points that many don't think about, is to ensure that you are diversified in terms of insurance companies. We have seen what happened during the financial crisis, when some insurance companies suffered much more than others. Imagine your insurance policies were all with that one insurance company that was most impacted by the crisis – how would you have felt then? Not a pleasant thought, I'm sure. So one of the best things you could help yourself with is to ensure that if you have more than one insurance policy, spread your risk and buy from different insurance companies!

Which Policies to Buy?

After reading the above, you probably know you should have life insurance policies, and the type of policies that suit you. However, what is stopping you is probably the cost of the insurance, as it is really difficult to put money into insurance when there are so many competing needs for cash.

What is life insurance really for? Insurance agents would tell you that it is really for protecting your earning potential, so that your dependants can be taken care of if the unfortunate happens to you. To arrive at an insurance coverage number, agents may extrapolate the cost of living and your earning potential over time, and try to forecast how much money you might need to provide for your family and/or retire on in the future. Without fail, the number that is arrived at is usually too large for most people to stomach. To achieve the said coverage, you would have to set aside a large amount of money for insurance premiums, probably when you can least afford it in your early career years. So how do you balance your need for protection and your competing need for cash when you are young and have so many things to buy and invest in?

The cheapest way to achieve high protection is via a Term Policy. But this does not have cash value, so many are reluctant to buy it as they think it is most likely "money down the drain". This is probably true, so would you rather die young and get the insurance payout? An insurance policy is really that, insurance. You do *not* hope for the insured scenario to come true most times. But if it does, then at least you are fully or partly compensated. This is usually a very hard sell to people, especially when money paid today is more precious than future dollars you might receive. In this case it is not even yourself who will be receiving the future dollars! But if one is serious about protecting one's earning potential and loved ones, then insurance is crucial to achieving that goal.

Given the reluctance to see one's premiums going down the drain, policies with cash value may be more appealing for people who see "forced savings" packaged with insurance as a slightly more palatable idea. However, policies with cash value are a lot more expensive than term policies. So the most common choice among the young is a combination – buy a little term policy, and buy a little whole life/endowment/investment-linked policy. That is a good start, as you are somewhat protected.

As you age, and your material and investment needs are somewhat more satisfied, you will probably add on other types of life policies along the way. And when you are reasonably comfortable financially, likely in your 40s, you will probably consider a Universal Life Policy too.

Most people beyond 55 would find it difficult to buy any insurance as their age would mean hefty premiums, making the "leverage" effect from an insurance policy's death benefit less lucrative. This is the most typical life cycle or profile of a person's encounter with life insurance.

How Much Insurance Coverage Do You Need?

This is more of an art than a science, as it depends on many variables, and these variables change over time. Some of these variables are the number of dependants, how much they need for college education, how many mortgages you have and the outstanding amount, what kind of lifestyle you/ your dependants lead, cost of living, and the list goes on. You would notice that all the above are difficult to give a straight-forward answer to, and most of them would be dependent on a set of other conditions, and all of them change over time!

From the perspective of retirement planning, you need a sum of money equivalent to 5–10 times your last drawn annual salary, as a rough guide. This need not all come from insurance with cash value obviously, and could be made up of other investments and savings that you have accumulated over the years. In many countries, less than 50% of the working population has life insurance. My guess is that a majority of those with life insurance tend to buy them to provide for their loved ones, and not so much for themselves. In other words, most would not depend on the life insurance cash values to provide for themselves in retirement years.

In Chapter 10 on Asset Allocation, I will be covering how to invest and plan for the future. Insurance is not an asset class that I have included in that discussion, for it is extremely illiquid and requires one to be very long-term (>12 years) to see positive returns. In my view, the better and more conservative way is to view insurance as more of a backup plan than an investment product by itself. Ideally, you don't want to depend on it for your retirement years, but use it as an insurance against your investment plan not working out!

If you agree with that view, then the type and amount of insurance you would need would be a combination of life coverage to provide for your dependants and cash value to supplement or act as insurance for your retirement funds. Given that, I would suggest that one should consider having a combination of term policy and policies with cash value.

Premium-first vs Coverage-first

In an ideal world, we would have enough cash to buy insurance to achieve both the right coverage and the desired cash value. But that is seldom the case in real life as we are usually constrained in terms of our cash resources. So should we then first consider the amount to be insured (coverage-first) or how much money to allocate to insurance products (premium-first)? This would determine the mix of term policies and cash value policies to buy.

(a) Coverage-first

If coverage is more important to you, then you should decide how much coverage you need, and then allocate cash to buy enough of the life coverage first. Start by evaluating the premium required to achieve 100% of coverage via a Term Policy. If the premium required is smaller than what you can afford or intend to set aside for insurance, then iteratively move some coverage from there to policies with cash value. Alternatively, you could also allocate any balance cash to other savings and investments products. Note that under the coverage-first model, one is unlikely to have much in savings/investment in insurance policies.

(b) Premium-first

In this case, one decides how much money to allocate to insurance first, and then decides how much of it should go to term policies and how much to policies with cash value. The coverage is thus derived from the mix that could be achieved from the premium allocation. My suggested split in terms of the mix of policies varies with the age of the insured:

Age of Insured	Term Policy	Policy with Cash Value
Below 30	50%	50%
30–40	40%	60%
Above 40	30%	70%

The proposed split takes into account one's earnings and free cash flow constraints at different life and career stages. It is a practical allocation giving adequate consideration and balancing the coverage and investment/savings angle. As the insured ages and becomes more comfortable financially, he will then be able to increase his insurance premium allocation and also the proportion to policies with cash value.

Conclusion

Insurance products are usually not thought of as investment products, and would normally not feature prominently in a book on investments. However, insurance is still a reasonably popular retail product, and because some policies accrue cash value, it is worth covering the topic here to be complete.

Like investment products, the variations are aplenty. Broadly speaking, the two types are term policies and policies with cash value. Policies with cash value could be seen as long-term investment products too because policy holders can choose to terminate the policies before maturity and monetise the cash value, though that is generally not recommended by most insurers.

In choosing a life policy, you should be clear with your objective and time horizon. Diversification of insurance companies should also be considered if you own more than one policy. To achieve a balance between life coverage and investment cash value, I recommend a mix of term policy and policies with cash value so as to help you grow your cash value while having some life protection.

Life insurance is crucial for estate planning. However, from an investment perspective, due to the very long-term commitment, long-term break-even and illiquidity, there may be better alternatives out there.

Part III

PUTTING IT ALL TOGETHER

CHAPTER 10

Asset Allocation

You might have heard of Asset Allocation in financial reporting or financial planning. It sounds big, complicated and scary, doesn't it? Most people think that they are not "rich" enough to need to think about Asset Allocation, and that it is the domain of millionaires and large funds. Here I will try to dispel the notion that Asset Allocation is only for the rich or the "big boys", and show you that it is really a concept that every individual who has investable funds should know and use to his or her advantage.

Asset Allocation, or AA for short, is merely a plan or strategy for how one should divide one's wealth or investable funds into different compartments or assets so as to earn a risk-balanced return to satisfy one's unique needs. Even if one has just say $100,000 in investable funds, one should still devise a plan for where this $100,000 is to be deployed. The earlier or younger one has a plan, the more likely one is able to grow one's funds in a meaningful and profitable trajectory.

Most literature on AA limits the allocation to just three

broad asset classes – Bonds, Equities and Cash. In the real world, there are a few more asset classes that could help diversify one's portfolio, and I will include one more – Physical Property, or Real Estate as it is more commonly known – in this chapter.

To ensure there is no ambiguity, this chapter will limit the discussion on AA to only investable cash. This would include physical property that one invests in, but exclude the home that one lives in. It also excludes the contributions that one makes into a pension, which cannot be accessed until one's retirement. Every country has its own unique pension scheme, and some have schemes that allow individuals to use the contributed funds to buy a home or even invest in equities, unit trusts, etc. However, as most returns generated from these funds cannot be converted to cash and used as income until one reaches retirement age, I will exclude discussion on them for simplicity.

Similarly, life insurance or endowment policies are also instruments many like to use for retirement planning or for a specific purpose like a child's education fund. These policies usually have maturity of 18 years or more, or only pay out when one dies. For an endowment policy used as a "bullet" fund which pays out when say a child turns 18 to fund the child's tertiary education, it functions like a forced savings plan. Similarly for a life policy, which only pays out when one dies (assuming one does not look to redeem the cash value accrued), the cash flow it generates benefits only the next generation or the beneficiary. These "forced savings plans" with lumpy cash flows have their uses, but generally they are difficult to incorporate in a relatively active AA strategy. In Chapter 9 on Insurance, I stated my preference for treating these insurance policies as a "fall-back plan". What I mean is that I would like to plan my AA without them. Should my AA result in less-than-expected returns, these insurance policies could be what I fall back on to "supplement" my needs.

Different Asset Classes

By now, you probably have a good idea of what is the investable universe available to you. Where do you start then? Most financial planners will start by asking you a few questions on:

- ◆ Age

- ◆ Family structure

- ◆ Income

- ◆ Risk appetite or tolerance

- ◆ Investment time horizon

- ◆ Investment objective

These are important questions to start with and not to be sniffed at. Yes they are boring, but they are part of an important and necessary process to go through in order for you to plan your financial future properly. I won't ask you these questions now, but I would like you to spend a few moments to think about them. These questions are best covered in a face-to-face setting since every individual is different and has his or her own unique circumstances.

Be careful if you come across online self-help portals that claim to be able to prepare an AA for you by merely asking a few simple questions. Whatever is recommended may or may not be most suited to you, as the recommendations are inevitably generic to a large extent. Asset Allocation is ideally an iterative process, both from a top-down perspective as well as from a bottom-up perspective. We will look into that in more detail later in this chapter.

For now, to help you understand more about AA, I will start with the most common AA concept, something you will hear all the time from asset allocators or financial planners:

◆ "More in Equities or higher-risk products if you are young and upwardly mobile"

◆ "More in Bonds or lower-risk products if you are near retirement age"

These are simple concepts to keep at the back of your mind and the reasons behind it are clear:

The younger you are, the more risks you can afford to take to grow your capital. Even if you are wrong in the short term, you have a lot more time to recover. If you are at or nearing retirement, you can't afford to take as much risks as you might not have enough time to see the next market recovery.

These are great concepts, but are they enough for you to now go away and implement them? These concepts are too high-level to implement for most retail investors. For example, you may have cash needs in a year's time for your daughter who is college-bound, and you would also like to plan for your retirement in about ten years' time. So how do you balance your coming cash needs with your longer-term plans? What should you be invested in now and for the future? What could you do with your existing investments, or what if your current live-in house is deemed an investment for you?

Real Estate as an asset class is gaining more prominence. It is probably more popular in Asia than in other parts of the world as most Asians prefer to own the home they live in. In addition, Asians like to invest in properties for capital preservation, inflation hedge, growth, rental income and/or passing on to the next generation. Whatever the reasons may be, as real estate is an asset class requiring large capital investment dollar-amount-wise, it is not possible to have a small allocation percentage-wise (e.g. 10% of investable capital of $300,000 is only $30,000, not enough in most developed countries requiring at least 20–30% in down-payment), unless of course one has several million dollars in investable capital.

While I stated upfront that I would not consider one's live-in house as an "investment", I do recognise that it could be monetised if one chooses to "downgrade" to a smaller apartment and free up cash for retirement. This could be one's plan, but like insurance, I would prefer to keep it as a backup. I would not advocate that one plans this in from the start, as one's quality of life may suffer with the downgrade. However, if one's AA were to yield lower-than-expected return, monetising the live-in house would be a possible safety net.

Cash can be thought of as the balancing item to ensure one's liquidity needs are met. In its simplest form, it could be just cash in a current account or time deposit. Depending on income and liquidity needs, we could improve the yield of cash or cash equivalents by taking small risks and sacrificing a little in liquidity.

There are other asset classes that more sophisticated and risk-loving investors like to dabble in. The two main ones are Foreign Exchange and Commodities. Foreign Exchange (FX) is among the favourites as a retail product when packaged in a structured investment; it can also be traded on a standalone basis but involves a lot more risks due to the high leverage. Commodities, covering anything from gold to orange juice, have attracted much attention in the recent past due largely to the growth in China and its consumption of all types of commodities. Because of the complexity of this asset class, most retail investors would be ill-equipped to trade commodities. The most commonly traded is gold, and that is also a popular product to be included in a structured investment.

For FX and Commodities, while they may be common and popular among retail investors, they are highly speculative and should never take up a significant weight in an one's AA plan, and so we will exclude them in this chapter. For the sophisticated active investors who insist on having them, I would recommend carving out a tiny portion, say no more than 3% of one's portfolio, to trade this. Alternatively, one could allocate a portion from the "cash" component to trading FX and Commodities.

Other less common asset classes meant more for the wealthy include Private Equity and Alternative Investments. Private Equity is simply a class of equity that is not publicly listed, hence the name. They are more commonly thought of as start-ups or in the dot-com days, the dot-com companies.

Nowadays Private Equity is used more broadly to include anything non-public, from small start-ups to large "unicorns" about to be listed in a public exchange.

Alternative Investments, or some call them Hedge Funds, are a different class of managed pools of money similar to Unit Trusts. The main difference is that they are typically highly leveraged and more sophisticated, many employing long-short strategies instead of most Unit Trusts' strategy of long-only. That means that besides owning an asset like stock, Hedge Funds could also borrow stocks they don't own for the objective of selling it, or shorting it. Hedge Funds are therefore a good "hedge" to the typical long-only funds as theoretically Hedge Funds should be able to profit from a down market as much as an up market.

Investments in Private Equity and Hedge Funds typically require large outlays of $100,000 or more, putting them out of the reach of most retail investors. The risks there are generally much higher than public equities and unit trusts, but with higher risks would also come potentially higher returns. As such, only for the ultra-HNWIs, I would recommend an allocation of no more than 10% into Private Equity and/or Hedge Funds.

Asset Allocation is not just for retirement planning. It can be used to plan for capital growth or cash needs even when one is in the prime of one's working career. In other words, one can have an AA plan when one starts working and generating an income, and gradually evolve the plan as one ages such that the AA plan could be used at retirement or for estate planning.

To make the following examples more relevant for readers who long for Real Estate in their portfolios, I have included Physical Property in the various Asset Allocation mixes. Let's examine how one really implements AA concepts in practice.

Examples of Asset Allocation Plans

Every individual is different. In trying to devise AA plans, it is important to understand every individual's unique needs and tailor something for that individual. Without the benefit of a face-to-face meeting, I can only give you a flavour of the thinking that should go into devising an AA plan.

To do that, I will cover AA plans for three different scenarios. They are by no means "model" AA portfolios, as there is nothing "model" about them and they pertain to three unique individual situations. What is important is to understand the thought process that goes into devising these plans, and adapt them to your own unique circumstances. Please consult a financial planner to draw up your own plan. The plans we will look at are for these three scenarios:

- ◆ For a young and upwardly mobile professional working adult in his/her late 20s or early 30s.

- ◆ For a person who has worked many years or is nearing retirement age or nearing his/her own desired age to "do my own thing". This person is likely to be in his/her late 30s, 40s or early 50s.

- ◆ For a retired person typically aged above 55 or a "retiring" one who is financially secure and would like to "do things that I like to keep busy".

I will cover each of the recommended AA strategies in broad terms. For detailed discussion on what each asset class entails, please refer to their respective chapters.

Plan 1:
For a young and upwardly mobile
professional working adult in
his/her late 20s or early 30s.

At this young age, you are likely to have a lot of cash needs. You are doing well in your career, have been promoted a couple of times over the years and are likely to get even higher in the corporate world in the next few years. You are looking to do one or more of the following: get married, start a family, buy an apartment, buy a car. All these are very demanding on cash needs.

Without proper advice, these needs usually lead to one of two types of "barbell" behaviour – the first being simply saving/accumulating cash and placing it in deposit accounts earning safe but meagre yield, and the other being to aggressively "punt" the available investable cash (or even leverage/borrow) so as to achieve desired returns sooner. Obviously these are two types of behaviour at extreme ends, and are exhibited by conservative investors and aggressive investors respectively.

There is no right or wrong investment style here, as it depends on a person's risk appetite and more importantly the person's ability to take a loss if it happens. It is only wrong when one chooses an investment portfolio that does not correspond to one's investment risk appetite and objective. Instead of choosing either end of the barbell approach,

HIGH NET WORTH INVESTING

there is a middle-ground. The example below is a case of the middle-ground that will better meet the needs of a typical young individual without taking excessive risks:

AA for a 30-year-old young professional with $100,000

Asset Class	Allocation	Remarks
Equities	70%	Strong emphasis on growth; high allocation here also means losses may mount in a bear cycle
Bonds	25%	Ensures some balance and capital preservation
Real Estate	0%	Working towards owning this asset to live in
Cash & Cash Equivalents	5%	Minimal cash requirement as salary is sufficient to meet daily needs

Here, you are a young working professional aged 30, earning a stable income which allows you to save a couple of thousand dollars a month. In the next three to five years, you are looking to buy an apartment of your own to live in and possibly also get married at the right time. You have accumulated savings of $100,000, which you are willing to risk part of in search of higher returns so that you can afford the downpayment on your dream apartment.

This is a portfolio geared for relatively aggressive growth, hence the high allocation to Equities. To provide for some stability in income, there is 25% allocated to Bonds. Due to this young person's limited near-term liquidity needs, only 5% is kept in Cash.

Plan 2:
For a person who has worked many years or is
nearing retirement age or his/her own desired age
to "do my own thing". This person is likely to
be in his/her late 30s, 40s or early 50s.

In this example, you are 45 and you have worked for over 20 years. You live in an apartment bought in your 30s, earning a salary that is comfortable enough to support yourself and your family. You would have accumulated some savings over the years, and have some experience with investing in asset classes like Equities. There is little immediate cash need as you still earn a decent salary, of which you are likely to save about 25–30%. Your financial obligations are limited to servicing your lived-in apartment's mortgage and your car loan, and these are comfortably covered by part of your salary.

You are looking for an investment strategy to grow your nest egg of $300,000 over the next ten years or so while you are still working, so you can be financially independent earlier.

AA for a 45-year-old working professional with $300,000

Asset Class	Allocation	Remarks
Equities	45%	A fairly large allocation for superior long-term returns
Bonds	20%	Ensures some balance and capital preservation
Real Estate	30%	Investment property for capital gains and inflation hedge
Cash & Cash Equivalents	5%	Minimal cash requirement as salary is sufficient to meet daily needs

Usually, at or near the peak of one's career and earning power, there is little cash or liquidity need on a monthly basis. This is a great time to be invested in very illiquid Real Estate. Due to the small investable cash base of $300,000, it is difficult to allocate a small percentage to Real Estate. Hence, an allocation to Real Estate necessitates a corresponding large reduction in Equities and a small reduction in Bonds. Here, 30% allocation to Real Estate for the portfolio of $300,000 is $90,000, just enough to pay for the down-payment on a flat in the range of $250,000 to $450,000. What investment property to buy depends on factors like rental yield, cash flow required for monthly mortgage servicing, etc.

As for Bonds and Cash, a 25% allocation to Bonds and Cash combined would provide a balance to the portfolio and also help the portfolio to weather unexpected volatility in Real Estate and Equities.

Plan 3:
For a retired person typically aged above 55 or a "retiring" one who is financially secure and would like to "do things that I like to keep busy".

You have done well in your career, and now at 60 years old you are going to retire from corporate life and pursue your life interests in business or leisure. You have saved well and followed a disciplined investment strategy to invest your spare cash over the years and accumulated quite a comfortable amount of $1,000,000. The apartment you live in is fully paid for. You no longer earn a fixed salary, but you will be receiving some annuity from your pension plan on a monthly basis. This annuity is usually barely enough for minimum living expenses, and you need a monthly income to supplement that in order to maintain your previous lifestyle. Given the extended life expectancy due to improvements in life sciences, you expect to live to at least 85 and so cannot afford to deplete your savings at all.

AA for a 60-year-old "retiring" person with $1 million

Asset Class	Allocation	Remarks
Equities	30%	Still a decent-sized allocation for superior long-term gains
Bonds	30%	Ensures some balance and capital preservation
Real Estate	30%	Investment property for capital gains, inflation hedge and income
Cash & Cash Equivalents	10%	Provides cash flow for emergency needs like medical and monthly spending

An equal allocation of 30% to Bonds and Equities means more than half the portfolio is allocated to relatively liquid publicly traded instruments. This is important because there is a 30% allocation to Real Estate, which is a highly illiquid asset class, and any downturn in property prices may take a long time to recover; in view of the investor's age, it is not advisable to be overly concentrated in this asset class. Besides, the 30% allocation to Real Estate for a portfolio of $1,000,000 now translates to $300,000, a rather sizable amount typically invested in one property only, so it is a rather concentrated bet.

If this was the same property valued originally at say $400,000 when you bought it at 45 and financed over 20 years at a rate averaging around 3% per annum, you would have paid up to about 75% of the original purchase price, or about $300,000 by now, to exactly the allocation I have suggested here. If this property had gone up by just 3% a year since you bought it, it would be worth about 55% higher, or $623,000 now. This gain in value does not sound like a lot compared to the $400,000 original property purchase price. Bear in mind, however, that your initial capital allocated to it 15 years ago was merely $90,000. If you compare the $223,000 gain to this $90,000, you have just gained almost 2.5 times your initial investment! Even when compared to the total amount paid over the years of $300,000, the percentage gain is still not to be sniffed at. The reason you have this outsized gain, if you haven't realised, is because Real Estate is effectively a leverage play due to mortgage!

You will notice from the above illustration that for Real Estate, I have only accounted for the amount you have contributed over the years ($300,000), and not the current market value ($623,000). I have chosen a more conservative approach. A more aggressive approach could be to use a fair percentage of the "mark-to-market" valuation of the property. Bear in mind that a mark-to-market approach may introduce much volatility into our AA model due to the leverage we employ. Also, remember that we may have to take a hefty discount to get out of such an illiquid asset class at short notice.

Allocation to Cash is higher at 10% as you would not have a fixed salary now. While you may have your annuity cash flow, emergency cash needs due to medical conditions, for example, tend to be more unpredictable, higher and lumpier.

The three examples above seek to provide a flavour of how one should think about Asset Allocation broadly.

Even with the addition of Real Estate to the mix, you would observe that the basic idea is about balancing risk versus returns, liquid versus illiquid assets, and ensuring one's cash needs can be met.

Top-Down vs Bottom-Up

You have just seen a top-down approach to Asset Allocation – top-down in the sense that we consider what assets are broadly suitable for you based on your profile like age and earning power. In practice, when we try to put in place our AA plans, we are still faced with many difficult choices. For example, within Stocks, what type of stocks should one buy – blue chips or growth stocks or speculative stocks? Within Bonds, should one be in Government bonds or Corporate bonds? For Cash, are there ways to enhance returns without sacrificing too much liquidity? The questions go on...

Top-down AA gives you a good guide on what you should have in your portfolio. The types of sub-assets you have within each asset class still depend chiefly on your risk appetite and needs. This is where bottom-up AA analysis is useful.

By bottom-up, we start by asking what one's investment objective is or what cash flow needs one has. We then choose the types of sub-assets within each asset class that could meet those needs, if possible. Very often, we will find that our targets for cash and liquidity needs are too high to be met. When that happens, we may have to alter the mix of sub-assets within each asset class, or even alter the weight of the asset allocation slightly while ensuring that the final AA mix is still within one's risk appetite.

This is an iterative process best done with an expert or a qualified financial planner. If this iterative process fails to come up with an AA plan that could meet one's cash and liquidity needs, then more often than not that is due to overly demanding needs and/or an insufficiently large investable pool of cash. In that case, it is important for the person to recognise early that his objectives cannot be met with an AA plan that matches his risk appetite, and he would have to lower his expectations accordingly. This is crucial, as this person would then have a concrete idea of what to expect from his portfolio and adjust his future plans early. This may mean a realisation that his dream car may not come in the next three years but in five years, or his plan for retirement can only start from 63, instead of 58. Best to know this now and plan for it than to be faced with a reality check when the time comes and one is less able to adapt.

To illustrate how this iterative process works, let's expand on the above example of the 45-year old and see how we could help him achieve his objectives.

In our conversation with this 45-year old gentleman, Mr Lee, we gathered the following additional information. Mr Lee is employed and earns a net (after pension contribution and tax) monthly salary of $14,000. He is married with one child aged 10. His wife is a homemaker.

Mr Lee and family live in an apartment bought in his mid-30s. The current market value of the apartment is $700,000, and his outstanding mortgage is $250,000. The monthly mortgage repayment for the next 20 years is $1,300 per month. He owns a family car, with loan repayment of $700 per month. This amount is expected to stay constant for the next 10 years minimally as Mr Lee would like to change to a new car whenever his car loan is fully paid. Excluding these two fixed loan repayments, Mr Lee's monthly family expenses add up to about $8,000. Mr Lee saves and invests the remaining $4,000 of his monthly salary.

Mr Lee hopes to be able to "retire" and do his own thing when he turns 55. As it is his choice to retire at 55 rather than the official retirement age, he will only retire if he can maintain his current lifestyle at that time. He would like to live solely on the income generated from his portfolio without running down that portfolio's capital value because he is not sure how long more he might live after 55. Thus he would like to know how much he needs to have in his portfolio in order for him to retire at 55 and how to allocate his assets to achieve that.

Let's examine the mathematics. In order to focus on this bottom-up process of AA and not get distracted by being overly accurate, let's assume for simplicity that Mr Lee's net income remains the same for the next 10 years, and we live in a world with no inflation. If Mr Lee wants to retire and live on income generated from his portfolio alone, his portfolio in 10 years' time must be large enough to generate at least $10,000 monthly to cover his housing loan, car loan and living expenses. That translates to $120,000 a year.

To generate that kind of annual income or yield, he needs $1 million in his portfolio generating 12% returns annually, or $2 million generating 6% yield. There are obviously other permutations, but this quick "sanity check" would reveal that based on past experience, an annual 12% return every year is probably not the most realistic. At the same time, 6% sounds like an achievable target. However, $2 million in 10 years sounds like mission impossible when Mr

Lee only has $300,000 now. So our target to grow Mr Lee's portfolio would have to target somewhere between one and two million. What we have done is get a rough idea of the target and challenge. Now we can focus on how we can grow Mr Lee's portfolio from the current $300,000 to somewhere near $2 million in 10 years if possible. Let's work through the numbers.

If we can grow his $300,000 portfolio by 8% every year for the next 10 years, after the first year it will be at $324,000. Mr Lee would also have saved $4000 × 12 or $48,000 in the year and put it into the portfolio for investment once a year. So at the end of Year 1, his total portfolio will be $372,000.

If we continue this math, at the end of Year 2, his total portfolio will be $449,760.

Year 3:	$533,741
Year 4:	$624,440
Year 5:	$722,395
Year 6:	$828,187
Year 7:	$942,442
Year 8:	$1,065,837
Year 9:	$1,199,104
Year 10:	$1,343,032

If we could structure his $300,000 portfolio to grow at 8% annually, and he saves $48,000 a year diligently, his investable portfolio will grow to over $1.3m in 10 years! Not bad at all, you think, but is it enough for Mr Lee to retire? That depends on what return we could generate from his portfolio after he retires. If we assume we could still consistently generate this 8% yield in cash for his spending infinitely after Mr Lee's retirement at end of Year 10, he would have $107,443 cash every year to spend, very close to the $120,000 that he needs. We have now further refined our target and have a >8% target return for Mr Lee's AA plan to work towards, so that he can have his $120,000 cash needs every year.

Let's now see if it is possible or how we could asset allocate to help Mr Lee make >8% a year from his portfolio. We suggested earlier his top-down AA to be:

Asset Class	Allocation	Remarks
Equities	45%	A fairly large allocation for superior long-term returns
Bonds	20%	Ensures some balance and capital preservation
Real Estate	30%	Investment property for capital gains and inflation hedge
Cash & Cash Equivalents	5%	Minimal cash requirement as salary is sufficient to meet daily needs

Now let's focus on getting the >8% return from the above allocation, and see what kinds of risks Mr Lee would have to take to achieve it. Top-down, considering what is possible within the realm of long-term average returns from each asset class, we could attempt to structure something based on the following return profile for each asset class:

Asset Class	Allocation	Expected return	Total % Return	Remarks
Equities	45%	12%	5.4%	Equity returns are wide-ranging, from stable blue chips to volatile growth stocks. We need returns to be high here to achieve the >8% target
Bonds	20%	5%	1%	Bond returns typically range from 2% for government bonds to above 10% for sub-investment grade junk bonds. Let's pick a balanced portfolio.
Real Estate	30%	6%	1.8%	Let's conservatively assume that the investment property is rented out and its rental exactly covers the interest portion of the mortgage. 6% return is from annual capital appreciation based on the capital invested only. If property is say 33% paid-up, an annual 2% appreciation for the property will equate to 6% return on the capital invested due to leverage.
Cash & Cash Equivalents	5%	2%	0.1%	Cash and money market instruments should be able to yield about 2% annually.
Total Expected % Return			8.3%	

It would seem that the top-down allocation is able to achieve an 8.3% total expected return annually. But what must we have in each of the asset classes to achieve that return? Is Mr Lee comfortable with the risks there? Let's look at each asset class from bottom-up now:

(a) Equities

To achieve a 12% return target for Equities, we need to have a rather aggressive allocation to growth stocks. Looking at historical returns of different types of stocks, a possible allocation could be 80% to growth stocks, and 20% to defensive blue chips. Whether this percentage allocation could achieve the 12% depends on which market one invests in. A qualified financial planner will be able to advise you, based on historical data combined with his and your views of the world equities markets in the future. If we have to invest in overseas markets to achieve this growth target, we will also have to consider the effect of Foreign Exchange on our returns.

Once the markets and sectors to be invested in are decided, we then have to decide whether to buy individual stocks, Exchange-Traded Funds (ETFs) or Unit Trusts in the respective sectors. Again, it is an iterative process to determine what and how much to invest in each of the selected instruments, making sure that the final outcome is in line with the investor's risk appetite.

(b) Bonds

In the current low-yield environment, achieving 5% is not an easy target. This implies more risks have to be taken, and that comes in two main forms in bonds – credit and tenure. In theory, Mr Lee could buy into long-tenure bonds that provide higher yields, as he has no short-term liquidity needs. However, he would also have to consider that bond prices would fall should interest rates rise from the current rock-bottom level. Mr Lee would also have to buy less-safe corporate bonds, as government bonds will not get him the high returns he needs.

If Mr Lee could gain access to retail bonds of smaller denominations in his home country and currency or bond ETFs, an allocation might be 80% to investment-grade ETFs or corporate bonds of tenure 3–5 years, and 20% to government bonds or ETFs of tenure at least five years.

If ETFs and retail bonds are not easily available, Mr Lee may consider buying Unit Trusts. There are many Unit Trusts that invest largely in investment-grade corporate bonds, with a small percentage (<30%) in high-yield bonds (also known as junk bonds) to enhance their returns. These types of Unit Trusts should be able to diversify the risks for Mr Lee as they usually limit the junk bonds to only a small part of the overall fund size.

(c) Real Estate

For most people, buying an investment property is usually the second biggest investment of their lives, after buying their own live-in home. Just as one would be extra careful in buying one's live-in home, one should also take one's time to decide on location, size, price range, etc. Work out one's financials, decide how much loan to take, over what period of time to service the mortgage, and find the best mortgage rates before committing to buy. This is an asset class requiring long-term commitment with high transaction costs, so do not rush it as mistakes are very costly.

In this example, Mr Lee would be renting out his investment property to offset part of his mortgage repayment, so he should get an apartment in a location that is easy to rent out. I recommend a property in the range of about $450,000, where Mr Lee would pay 20% down-payment and borrow the remaining in a mortgage loan to be repaid over the next 20 years. At a mortgage rate of 3%, monthly repayment would be about $2,000. If the property can be rented out at $800 net per month (after service charges, sinking fund contributions, taxes, etc.), the balance $1,200 would be coming from Mr Lee's monthly savings of $4,000, which is exactly 30%.

This would be a perfect match with our AA plan, and a sustainable plan to finance the property. Mr Lee could adjust the target property price range depending on his down-payment terms, his mortgage tenure and rate, and also the potential rental income. If Mr Lee is buying a property without rental income, for example a property under construction for the next three years, he may have to buy a lower-priced property so that he can finance the property for the first few years while keeping the total allocation to Real Estate within the 30% as planned.

As we assume that Mr Lee is only putting down 20% of the property value and financing 80%, a 1.2% annual appreciation of the property will translate to a 6% gain on his invested capital, due to the 5-times leverage. Appreciation of 1.2% per annum certainly sounds like an achievable target, probably even bordering on being conservative.

(d) Cash and Cash Equivalents

Given the above suggested allocations, which are all in medium to long-term investments, we need to keep some in cash or cash-liked products to ensure Mr Lee has access to liquidity in case of unforeseen circumstances.

I recommend a 30–40% allocation to a savings account, and the balance to Time Deposits or Structured Deposits. Most banks have savings accounts or statement accounts that pay a small interest rate; keep a balance there that is enough to cater to urgent liquidity needs. For the rest, put it in a series of Time Deposits or low-risk principal-protected Structured Deposits so that the maturity dates are spread out to enhance the liquidity position.

Refining the Asset Allocation Plan

We now have a complete Asset Allocation plan, right down to the specific instruments Mr Lee could use to implement it. Very often, investors have preferences and dislikes. What is Mr Lee's risk appetite? What are his preferences like? Do they match with what is proposed? Is Mr Lee happy with the portfolio and reasonably confident that the risks taken will give him a good chance of achieving his target returns and objectives eventually? That is really the key as he is the one who needs to be comfortable with it for it to work for him.

If our portfolio could indeed churn out the expected 8.3% return every year for the next 10 years, Mr Lee's portfolio would grow to $1,371,235 at the end of the 10th year. If we could continue generating 8.3% after the 10th year, Mr Lee would have an annual return of $113,813 to spend, pretty close to his target of $120,000!

At this point, Mr Lee must realise that these are all expected returns based on past experiences as well as our best educated guess going forward. Things seldom work out as planned, and his portfolio may be worth more or less at the end of the 10th year. As our current proposed AA plan already falls short of his required target portfolio size to generate an income of $120,000 per year after the 10th year, Mr Lee would have to make several decisions. Some questions that he should ask himself include:

- ◆ Am I comfortable with the broad asset allocation and the selected sub-asset classes?

- ◆ Am I prepared to increase the proportion of risky assets to improve my expected returns or consider reducing it if I am already not comfortable?

- ◆ Am I prepared to change my expectations/target of $120,000 per year?

Depending on how Mr Lee answers the questions, the financial planner's job would be to go back to the drawing board, and adjust the AA plan. This would largely be done from a bottom-up perspective, while always cross-checking from a top-down perspective that whatever AA plan devised would be appropriate for his profile and matches Mr Lee's risk appetite with his return expectations.

It is possible that after going through the above iterative process, the risk appetite still cannot match up to the returns required. If that happens, then the responsible thing for the financial planner to do would be to advise the investor to lower his expectations and adjust his future plans, instead of feeding the investor with a portfolio of higher risks that he is not ready to stomach.

Alternatively, one could also consider the "fall-back" plans that the investor may have. I mentioned a couple earlier, like insurance policies with cash value and downgrading one's live-in house. If really necessary, they could be factored into the AA plan, but I emphasise that they should ideally be Plan B and should not be used if possible.

Reviewing the Asset Allocation Plan

An AA plan is not a static plan where one just does it once and revisits it after ten years. It should be a "living" plan that is reviewed periodically to ensure it is current and relevant to one's circumstances and the global environment. A suggested frequency for a quick review of market and performance is every quarter to half-yearly, a mid-term review of effectiveness every 2–2.5 years, and a complete review every 5–8 years.

It is important to review the AA plan as we live in a world that changes in a flash. While we should be patient and allow time for our portfolio to perform over time, we should also not be stubborn or stupid to stick to a plan if the macro environment has clearly changed. Our own individual circumstances also change periodically. When a major change happens, for example if one is retrenched or promoted, it is also an opportune time to review the AA plan to adjust for the new circumstances.

Strategic vs Tactical Asset Allocation

Fund management houses that have Asset Allocation plans tend to have both a Strategic Asset Allocation plan (SAA) and a Tactical Asset Allocation plan (TAA). Depending on the type of organisation, SAA tends to be very long-term, typically way beyond one year. TAA is obviously tactical moves around the SAA, and this is done regularly.

From an individual investor perspective, SAA is like a five-year plan. This five-year SAA plan is similar to what we arrived at in the above example for the 45-year-old Mr Lee. After numerous iterations, we would have a plan for Mr Lee to execute, and he would typically put in place this plan as soon as practicable.

However, in real life, it is usually not easy to quickly implement the AA plan, especially when it involves illiquid asset classes like real estate. When that happens, it is good discipline to have a TAA during the interim implementation period to guide us. For example, depending on when Mr Lee thinks he will be buying his investment property, he would have to decide whether to place the money in a money market fund, time deposit, cash or some other less liquid asset class like equities or bonds.

TAA could also be used to express a view for the short term, while keeping the SAA untouched. For example, if Mr Lee felt that the US economic cycle is about to turn, and the US stock market's tech stocks are over-valued, he could choose to take profit on them and/or move the exposure into more defensive utilities stocks. Now this is obviously rather speculative, and it is not recommended for most retail investors other than the most sophisticated. The idea of TAA should ideally be used less for speculative reasons and more for short-term adjustments of position. When retail investors think of doing short-term adjustments, it is crucial that they keep in mind what the SAA is, and what they are doing is just a short-term move. They should have a well-thought-out plan to realign their portfolio back to their SAA plan before doing any short-term TAA. The last thing we want is for a short-term trade to become a long-term SAA trade simply because it was a bad investment and the investor could not bear to cut his losses!

Conclusion

Asset Allocation is a big topic, but it does not need to be complicated. Every individual with investable funds should make an AA plan, irrespective of how old he or she is. An AA plan could be as simple as having just one or two asset classes, or as complex as one wants it to be, including Foreign Exchange, Commodities, Alternative Investments and Private Equity. The most important thing is to think about it, plan for it, and execute it to achieve a return that corresponds to one's risk appetite and needs.

In making an AA plan, most literature covers the top-down approach based on a very general set of criteria like a person's age and financial situation. The top-down approach unfortunately does not easily translate to actionable tasks and is usually too high-level and does not consider the practical difficulties in implementation. This is when a bottom-up approach could complement it. To be effective, one should do asset allocation in both top-down and bottom-up directions iteratively until one reaches a concrete plan that is actionable and consistent with one's risk appetite and return expectations.

Having an AA plan early will give you the best chance of growing your nest egg, due to the amazing power of compounding. The plan does not guarantee that you make more money, but at least you will be actively working towards a future state that you hope for. Not making a plan is basically leaving everything to chance, and blindly hoping for the best. Remember to always review your plan along the way to ensure it stays relevant to your needs.

Wait no more, start a simple Asset Allocation plan now!

ABOUT THE AUTHOR

SAM PHOEN is a seasoned financial markets practitioner with over 20 years of experience. His working career has included 16 years in the Government of Singapore Investment Corporation (GIC), where he was the deputy department head of the Foreign Exchange Department when he left to join a large Singapore-based hedge fund as a senior macro portfolio manager. He then had over seven years with Australia and New Zealand Banking Group (ANZ), where he was mainly based in Shanghai managing the Global Markets business for ANZ China.

Sam is a graduate of the National University of Singapore, and is a Chartered Financial Analyst (CFA). Sam was also a board director for CFA Singapore for three years before he left to work in ANZ China.

A keen golfer and seasoned investor, Sam has vast experience in trading many products and instruments for the firms he has worked for as well as for himself.